TANZANIA

Jay Heale

MARSHALL CAVENDISH

New York • London • Sydney

Reference edition published 1998 by
Marshall Cavendish Corporation
99 White Plains Road
Tarrytown
New York 10591

PUB 3/30/98

© Times Editions Pte Ltd 1998

Originated and designed by
Times Books International, an imprint of
Times Editions Pte Ltd

Printed in Singapore

Library of Congress Cataloging-in-Publication Data:
Heale, Jay.
      Tanzania / Jay Heale.
        p. cm.—(Cultures of the World)
      Includes bibliographical references and index.
      ISBN 0-7614-0809-6 (lib. bdg.)
      1. Tanzania—Juvenile literature. I. Title. II. Series.
DT438.H34 1998
967.8—dc21   97–42180
                     CIP
                     AC

INTRODUCTION

TANZANIA IS EVERYONE'S popular picture of Africa. It has endless sunbaked plains, thorn trees, wild animals, and Masai warriors who still wear traditional clothes. Yet it is also a country as varied as can be, both in landscape and in people. Snowcapped mountains, sun-dried plains, rocky cliffs plunging into deep lakes, and elegant, palm-fringed beaches are all found in Tanzania. It is a place of fascinating history reaching back to habitation by prehistoric humans. From the spice islands of the Indian Ocean to the refugee camps by the Great Lakes, from Makonde carvers on the Mozambique border to prehistoric footprints near Mount Kilimanjaro, there lives a proud nation of endlessly varied people struggling to combat the old scourges of Africa: drought, ill-health, food shortages, and poverty. Their history is a fight for independence and then economic survival. Yet they are a democracy and at peace. That, in Africa, is no small boast.

CONTENTS

Masai child holding a goat.

CONTENTS

An old-style dhow off the coast of Mafia Island.

GEOGRAPHY

TANZANIA, THE LARGEST COUNTRY IN EAST AFRICA, covers 364,900 square miles (945,090 square km) including its offshore islands of Zanzibar, Pemba, and Mafia. It is bigger than Kenya and Uganda put together, and half the size of Texas. It is bordered by eight countries: to the north, Kenya and Uganda; to the west, Rwanda, Burundi, and the Democratic Republic of Congo; to the south, Zambia, Malawi, and Mozambique. To the east lies the Indian Ocean.

Most of Tanzania is high, hot plateau land over 3,000 feet (1,000 m) above sea level, lying between the Indian Ocean on the east and the plunging line of rift valley lakes to the west, with more rift valley depressions through the center. Its terrain includes the highest mountain in Africa, Mount Kilimanjaro and the deepest lake, Lake Tanganyika. As with many African countries, the ability of the land to produce food is dwindling steadily. Much of what was once savannah and scattered bush is now turning into semidesert. Yet it is home to a spectacular array of wildlife.

Left: **Wide savannah plains have only a few, scattered acacia trees.**

Opposite: **Every year, thousands of flamingos use Lake Natron as a breeding ground.**

7

There are old African stories about a great flood that swallowed up plains once rich in cattle. These stories may refer to the way that rift lakes, such as Lake Tanganyika, were formed.

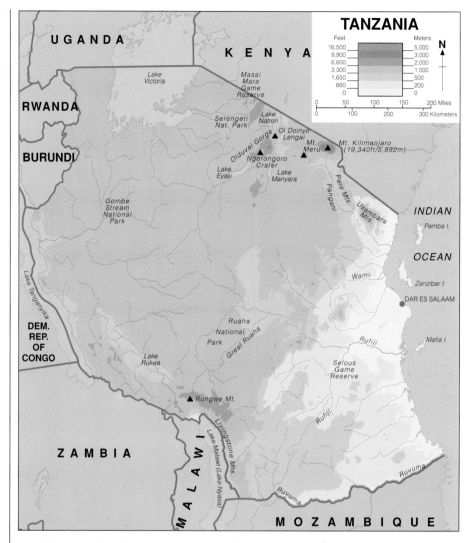

RIFT VALLEYS

The Great Rift Valley is an important geological feature in East Africa. It is made up of a series of fault lines caused by volcanic activity and stretches over 6,000 miles (9,650 km) from Syria and the Jordan valley to Lake Malawi at Tanzania's southern border. Water has filled some depressions creating a series of lakes. There are two rift valley branches in Tanzania: the western branch includes Lakes Tanganyika and Malawi; the eastern branch extends through Kenya to Lakes Natron and Eyasi and beyond.

LAKE TANGANYIKA, a rift valley lake, is the world's longest freshwater lake, and so deep as well (4,710 feet/ 1,435 m) that it contains seven times the amount of water in Lake Victoria, the world's second largest freshwater lake. Lake Tanganyika is home to 250 species of fish, seven species of crab, and the eastern aquatic cobra, a unique snake that fishes by day in the lake and sleeps on the rocks at night.

LAKE VICTORIA

The northwest corner of Tanzania is occupied by a large part of Lake Victoria, which it shares with Uganda and Kenya. More like an inland sea, Lake Victoria is so large that it has its own local climate (usually grey and humid). It is almost 27,000 square miles (70,000 square km) in area. Its southern waters provide Tanzania with fresh fish, a ferry route to Uganda, numerous small islands, and an extensive fertile shoreline that is heavily populated. Rapidly spreading hyacinth weed has become a problem in some areas of the lake, unfortunately. The dense weed blocks sunlight, which results in many fish dying. Yet Lake Victoria continues to be one of the largest sources of fish in Africa.

RIVERS

The major rivers of Tanzania are the Rufiji, the Ruvuma, the Wami, and the Pangani. All these rivers drain into the Indian Ocean. The Rufiji River is one of the great rivers of Africa, looping its way toward the sea, where it becomes choked by mangrove forests. It is wide and dangerous when it floods. Several smaller rivers drain into the rift valley basins.

Ha fishermen, who live on the shore of Lake Tanganyika, attract small *dagaa* fish on moonless nights using lights suspended on their boats.

To the Luo people of Kenya, Lake Victoria is known as Nam Lolwe, *"Lake without end."*

9

Ol Doinyo Lengai is known as the "Mountain of God" to the Masai.

VOLCANOES AND MOUNTAINS

The volcanic forces that formed the rift valleys are still active today; there are many active or semi-active volcanoes in the area. At 19,340 feet (5,892 m), Mount Kilimanjaro, once an active volcano, is the highest point in Africa. The mountain rises straight from the plains to snowcapped peaks. The southeastern slopes receive a considerable amount of rain and are very fertile. The Chaga people, who live on the slopes of Mount Kilimanjaro, grow a variety of crops. Coffee, in particular, grows very well in the volcanic soils. The mountain is also popular with climbers and has drawn many tourists to Tanzania. The higher of the two peaks, Kibo, is now named Uhuru (Freedom) Point.

Ol Doinyo Lengai, to the west of Mount Kilimanjaro, is still an active volcano. It pours out spurts of black lava that turn white within two days because contact with moisture in the air converts most of it to crystals of sodium carbonate, commonly known as washing soda. Many of the surrounding lakes have high amounts of soda as a result. The volcano last erupted in 1966, when a column of gas and cinders shot 5,000 feet (1,500 m) into the air.

The huge Ngorongoro Crater is part of the mountain chain including Ol Doinyo Lengai. It is the world's largest "caldera" or volcanic depression, enclosing an area of 100 square miles (260 square km). The land in the area used to belong to the Masai until they signed away their rights, but they still graze their cattle there.

"As wide as all the world, great, high and unbelievably white in the sun."

—Ernest Hemingway,
on Mount Kilimanjaro

THE PEAKS OF MOUNT KILIMANJARO

Mount Kilimanjaro (known affectionately as "Kili") has two peaks, Kibo and Mawenzi. In the Chaga language these names describe the peaks' appearance—the first as being "spotted" and the second as "having a broken top." According to a Chaga legend, there were once two sisters who were both the same height. However, Mawenzi was lazier than her sister Kibo and used to take her food to avoid having to cook herself. Kibo finally became angry one day and beat Mawenzi on the head with her wooden ladle. And that, they say, is why the sister peak is lower and has bumps on its head!

Mount Meru, at 14,980 feet (4,564 meters), is the second highest mountain in Tanzania. Both Mount Kilimanjaro and Mount Meru are part of the northern chain of mountains known as the Pare and Usumbara ranges which extend from the northern coast in a southeast to northwest direction. Mountains in southern Tanzania include the Livingstone Mountains as well as Rungwe Mountain.

Mafia Island lies off the east coast of Tanzania and is thinly populated. Its clear waters are rich with corals. Plans are under way to turn it into a marine park.

THE CENTRAL PLATEAU

One word describes the central and western plains of Tanzania—"vast." They cover more than one-third of the country and are hot, baked dry, fairly flat, and in places more vast and barren than words or pictures can convey. This is grassland country (savannah), with scattered thorny trees. In the dry season the area becomes semidesert.

EASTERN COAST

Nearly all of the eastern coastline has unspoiled, white-sand beaches, shaded by palms, overlooking warm turquoise waters. The sea teems with marine life, at least where the reefs have not been destroyed by dynamite fishing.

Zanzibar and Pemba are two islands that lie off the coast of the mainland. They are made of coralline rock and are mostly low-lying. Zanzibar Island is 53 miles (85 km) long and 12 miles (19 km) wide. It is rich with clove and other spice plantations and groves of coconut palms.

CLIMATE

Tanzania has three main climatic zones: the hot, steamy coastal strip, the dry central plateau, and the semi-temperate mountains. Along the coast (as well as beside Lakes Malawi and Tanganyika) it is humid for most of the year, day and night, relieved only by sea breezes. On the higher inland plains it is hot and dry, though much cooler at night. In most of the highlands it is warm during the day and cold at night.

The equator crosses midway through Kenya, to the north of Tanzania. This means that it is hot all year round, with hardly any difference between summer and winter. About half of Tanzania receives less than 30 inches (750 mm) of rainfall each year. The central plateau gets under 20 inches (500 mm) a year in a rainy season between December and May and loses much of this through evaporation caused by the continual heat. On the coast, rainfall is heavier. Nearly all the precious rainfall comes between March and May, a time known as the "long rains." There are lighter "short rains" during November and December.

The varied topography of Tanzania results in an unpredictable climate and rainy seasons that vary in length and intensity in different parts of the country.

TSETSE FLY

This is the name for bloodsucking insects (*Glossina morsitans* in Tanzania) found mostly in central African countries. Their bite transmits the disease called sleeping sickness, which affects both humans and animals such as cattle, horses, and goats. Many of the *miombo* ("mee-OM-bo") woodland areas in southern, central, and western Tanzania are infested with tsetse fly and as a result are very thinly populated by humans.

FLORA

The baobab tree is unmistakable with its enormous trunk, which can grow to 30 feet (9 m) in diameter. Baobab trees are pollinated by bats and live up to 2,000 years.

The plant life of Tanzania varies from coconut palms and mangroves on the coast to the flat-topped thorn trees of the inland plains. The two main types of tree cover in Tanzania are the dry *miombo* woodlands in the southern and western regions, which consist of a sparse cover of deciduous trees with a few baobab trees, and *montane* (typical mountain forest) on the foothills of the northern mountains, where there is higher rainfall. On the savannah plains there are only occasional thorny acacia varieties, including the yellow-fever tree that often grows near water. Figs and tamarinds sprout along the watercourses. After the rains, flowers sprout quickly, including different varieties of African violets.

POACHING

The desire for conservation in Tanzania has been accompanied by the sharp awareness that tourists will pay a lot of money to view wildlife reserves. Unfortunately, the establishment of reserves has meant that the surrounding human populations have been deprived of hunting grounds. With a growing population, there is an increasing need for food. Poaching for elephant ivory and rhino horn also became a significant problem when the market for these products started to grow. In the 1970s about 500 black rhino lived in Serengeti Reserve; by 1986 there were fewer than 20. In the Selous Game Reserve, nearly 20,000 elephants were killed for their ivory over a couple of years in the 1980s. Elephant poaching continues to be a big problem today throughout the reserves.

Gombe Stream National Park is famous as a chimpanzee sanctuary and for the research done there by Dr. Jane Goodall.

FAUNA

Over 80 species of large mammals are indigenous to Tanzania, including wildebeest, zebra, giraffes, elephants, rhino, lions, and leopards. On riverbanks and lakeshores, crocodiles and hippos are common. Dugong and giant turtles live along the coast. There are over a thousand bird species in the country—including vultures, nature's clean-up specialists, that clear the plains of animal corpses which would otherwise rot. Many of the animals are specially protected, either through the many designated wildlife parks or through specific measures against poaching of animals such as rhino and elephants.

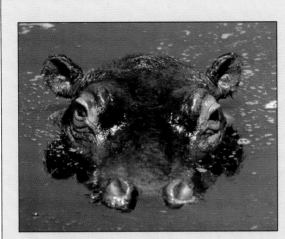

NATIONAL PARKS

Almost a quarter of Tanzania's countryside is set aside as protected wildlife areas. There are huge "wide-screen" winners such as Ngorongoro and Serengeti, with an annual migration of more than two million animals, as well as other smaller sanctuaries such as Gombe Stream National Park, Ruaha National Park, Rungwa Reserve, and Manyara National Park.

SERENGETI NATIONAL PARK In this park, which is linked with the Masai Mara Game Reserve in neighboring Kenya, there live well over a million wildebeest, perhaps 200,000 zebra, and thousands of giraffes, elephants, lions, and different species of antelope. The land, an area about the size of Connecticut, was set aside in 1940 with the intention of preserving the already fast disappearing wildlife. Its landscape varies from extensive grassland plains and savannah to more wooded areas in the west.

NGORONGORO CONSERVATION AREA This reserve contains a nearly circular volcanic crater, or caldera, 12.4 miles (20 km) across and surrounded by rock walls some 2,000 feet (600 m) high. Contained within this World Heritage site, the animals live wild—elephants and elands, hyenas and zebra, leopards and cheetahs and lions, even a few carefully monitored black rhino. Ostrich and crowned cranes stalk over the grassland, and the waters of Lake Magadi are often pink with flamingos.

SELOUS GAME RESERVE Claiming to be the world's largest game reserve, Selous ("se-LOO") is 21,000 square miles (54,400 square km) of virtually untouched Africa in southeastern Tanzania. The magnificent Rufiji River loops its way through the reserve. Only the northern tip has been explored and even the rangers can only give wild guesses on how many thousands of elephants, wildebeest, buffalo, antelope, or hippos the reserve contains.

SERENGETI MIGRATION

The north of Tanzania is one of the few remaining areas in Africa where natural annual migration takes place. During the early months of the year, half a million wildebeest calves are born in the rich volcanic plains around the Ngorongoro Crater. When the dry season starts in June, the grass dies and most animals migrate north to the Serengeti National Park where it is wetter and tall savannah grasses grow. Some two hundred thousand zebra lead the way, cropping the coarse tops of the long grass. As many as a million and a half wildebeest follow, feeding on the exposed succulent leaves and cropping the grass short, but leaving enough for the Thompson's gazelles that follow. Over two million animals in all migrate, their urge to migrate so strong that the herds ignore predators: crocodiles in the rivers they swim across and many carnivores (lions, cheetahs, leopards, wild dogs, hyenas, and jackals) on land. By September the herds are usually 500 miles (800 km) to the north, feeding in the Masai Mara Game Reserve inside the border of Kenya. When the rainy season starts in December, the herds head south to where the nutritious new grass will provide the right grazing for next year's calves.

Animals know no borders—the wildebeest migrate north annually from Ngorongoro Crater and Serengeti National Park in Tanzania to the adjoining Masai Mara Game Reserve in Kenya.

Much of Zanzibar's historic area, Stone Town, a maze of twisting, narrow streets, is still preserved. Many buildings are built of coral stone.

CITIES

The majority of Tanzanians live in rural areas; only about 15% of the population lives in the cities. Of these, one-third, or more than a million, reside in the capital city of Dar es Salaam on the coast. It is the starting point, by road, rail, or air, to the rest of Tanzania. "Dar," as locals call it, is not a particularly picturesque city. It is often hot and humid, though there can be cool sea breezes some parts of the year. In recent years many of the roads have been paved and the city is much cleaner, but it still has poor water, electricity, and sewage services. The outer perimeters of Dar es Salaam are no more attractive than those of other major African cities: a sprinkling of industrial works mixed with suburbs of shanty-lined alleys. Lines of washing hang from the balconies of dusty tenement blocks. The city, however, is alive with a colorful and varied population.

In 1862, Sultan Majid of Zanzibar found a fishing village slightly south of Zanzibar, on the mainland, where there was a natural harbor. He encouraged its use as a trading center. Four years later, he built himself a "haven of peace," *Dar es Salaam* , in the shape of a coral palace where he hoped to relax from his troubled reign on Zanzibar. The place deserved its name. Some 30 years later, it became the capital of German East Africa and it has been regarded as the capital city ever since—even though the Tanzanians are trying to transfer the seat of government inland to Dodoma.

Zanzibar Island lies just off the east coast of Tanzania. It has its own history and culture and in many ways is independent of the mainland. The capital of Zanzibar Island is the town of Zanzibar itself. Most of its population is Muslim. Zanzibar has grown a lot recently—this is putting heavy pressure on its infrastructure such as water services and roads.

Overlooking the sea in Zanzibar is the House of Wonders and the People's Palace, each of which was, in its time, the official residence of the Sultan of Zanzibar.

Dar es Salaam is important as a harbor city.

HISTORY

TANZANIA HAS SOME OF THE EARLIEST EVIDENCE of the origins of humankind. It was at Olduvai Gorge, on the edge of Serengeti National Park, that the famous scientists Louis and Mary Leakey discovered in 1959 the remains of human-like creatures nearly two million years old. Dr. Leakey named his first find "Handy Man," *Homo habilis,* as the evidence showed this man to be the earliest known to have used tools. Later, in 1978, Mary Leakey found 3.6-million-year-old footprints that proved these prehistoric beings had walked upright.

Little is known about the earliest inhabitants of Tanzania, though they were probably hunters and gatherers. By about 3,000 years ago the land was peopled by herders from the Ethiopian region and by Bantu-speakers of West African origin. These early herders evolved a system of local chiefs and councils, and in the central highlands they continued their customs in spite of the growing influence of outsiders along the coast.

Tanzania's more recent history has been primarily one of trade. The Phoenicians explored the east coast of Africa as early as 600 B.C. and it seems likely that they came to Tanzania. Certainly the Romans knew of Mount Kilimanjaro and the Great Lakes. The coast had trading contacts with Arabia from the 1st century A.D. and by A.D. 800 many traders had settled on the coastlands of Tanzania. Later the area attracted the attention first of the Portuguese, and then the Germans and British. Independent since 1961, the country is now struggling to overcome its economic problems.

Above: **Old Stone Town, Zanzibar. Zanzibar's economic power was once so great that it was said, "When the flute is played in Zanzibar, they dance at the Lakes."**

Opposite: **The old fort in Zanzibar.**

From the large quantity of Chinese pottery fragments discovered, historians conclude that Pangani, on the east coast of Tanzania, must have had trade links with the Far East.

TRADERS ARRIVE

Traders in small boats were coming across the Indian Ocean as early as the 1st century A.D. and became regular visitors to the eastern coast of Tanzania around A.D. 800. They came from Arabia, Persia, and India and settled in the coastal areas. They called it "Land of Zinj," meaning Land of Blacks. They were joined around 400 years later by the Shirazis, who were originally from Persia. Many married the local Africans and this was the beginning of the Swahili people—their language, Kiswahili, would eventually be spoken throughout East Africa.

THE COASTAL CITIES

Coastal cities grew and flourished, gaining their power and glory from the Indian Ocean trade. Pangani exported ivory, tortoiseshell, coconut oil, and rhino horns as early as the 2nd century B.C. Then, under Shirazi control, Pangani found improved fortune selling slaves and planting groves of coconut palms. Pangani's story was typical of many such medieval towns perched on the Indian Ocean, looking inland for the goods for trade and yet dependent on the distant country from which they had been colonized.

KILWA

In the 12th century, Kilwa was the most important city in East Africa until Mombasa (in modern Kenya) grew to greater importance. Kilwa was the main source of gold in the medieval world for over 200 years. The famed Moroccan traveler, Ibn Battuta, visited Kilwa in 1131 and declared that it was "among the finest and most substantially built in the world." It was subdued by the Portuguese and later sacked by a group called the Zimba in 1587. Now, mostly impressive ruins of palaces and mosques remain.

THE PORTUGUESE

The Portuguese, under Vasco da Gama, arrived at the end of the 15th century. The Portuguese sailors, on the way to and from India for spices, were doubtless impressed by the size and civilized standards of the east coast cities of Africa, but also considered them a source of trading competition that needed to be destroyed. They ruthlessly subdued Kilwa and Mombasa (in Kenya), virtually destroying the gold trade and showing no apparent interest in the interior of Africa.

The Portuguese overlords preferred exacting tribute to permanent settlement, though they did establish some trading centers around Lake Tanganyika. After some troubled times with Turkish pirates and increasing numbers of British ships, the Portuguese left. Hastening their departure were traders and raiders from Oman (on the eastern tip of Arabia) when the coastal Arabs formed an alliance with the sultan from Muscat, Oman. French interest in eastern Africa was also aroused in the 1700s. The Arab traders moved into the weakened towns and established Omani Arab governors. The important town of Kilwa itself finally submitted in 1787.

Although the slave market in Zanzibar was closed in 1873, it took another 50 years or so to wipe out slavery from the mainland.

IN THE INTERIOR

Unobserved by the marauding foreigners on the coast, changes in the power structure were taking place far inland around the 18th century. Groups such as the Nyamwezi and Hehe people began moving northeast and forming new chiefdoms such as the Chaga on Mount Kilimanjaro and the powerful kingdom of Usambara. This coastward movement was made more attractive by the development of trade. As news of these trade goods spread in the interior, fresh trade routes opened up toward Lake Tanganyika and the Haya kingdoms west of Lake Victoria. The separate threads of development of the coast and the interior began to be woven together.

The effect of the slave trade on East Africa must not be underestimated. While Arabs and Swahilis made fortunes from slave trading, the Nyamwezi and the Yua established their own power bases by providing porters and organizing the expeditions for slaves and ivory. The wholesale capture of hundreds of thousands of Africans left areas virtually uninhabited. Various warring groups then fought over the land.

SULTAN SAYYID SAID AND ZANZIBAR

The increasing value of the trade in gold, ivory, and slaves caused Sayyid Said, the Sultan of Muscat (Oman) in the Arabian peninsula, to look more carefully at the islands on the East African coast. He captured Pemba and Zanzibar and in 1832 moved his capital to Zanzibar, quite probably because it was a far more pleasant place in which to live than dusty Oman, but also so that he could gain control of coastal towns such as Bagamoyo through which the slave trade passed. By 1840 some 40,000 slaves a year were passing through the slave markets of Zanzibar.

The increasing call for slaves and ivory caused Arab and Swahili traders to search far inland, opening up the interior. After gold was discovered in North America and Australia, the mines in central Africa became less important. There were other profitable goods instead. Sultan Said encouraged the planting of cloves on Zanzibar and Pemba, and his Zanzibari traders also made fortunes from gum copal (a resin used in making varnishes and lacquers). White traders from Europe and the Americas came to buy in Zanzibar.

Sultan ibn Said Barghash was the son of Sultan Sayyid Said. His powers were greatly diminished when Germany and Britain claimed his lands.

THE SLAVE TRADE

Portugal was the first European nation to meet its needs for cheap labor by using slaves. By 1460 it was importing some 700 slaves a year from trading posts on the African coast. Arab traders made fortunes shipping slaves from Africa to Arabia, Iran, and India. However, when Britain abolished the slave trade in 1807 and the United States in the following year, the supply of slaves from West Africa to British colonies and the United States almost ceased. That made the East African slave markets supplying the Islamic world to the east even more prosperous.

THE SCRAMBLE FOR AFRICA

Toward the end of the 19th century, the European nations stopped sailing around the coast and turned their eyes on the huge, so far uncolonized, interior of Africa. They sent expeditions to claim, and if necessary conquer, territories to add to their growing empires in a disorganized first-come-first-grab procedure that is often called "the Scramble for Africa."

The British Consul in Zanzibar, John Kirk, helped to end the slave trade in Zanzibar and also increased British influence in the area through the Arabs. In 1884 Dr. Carl Peters of Germany made a series of treaties with a number of inland chiefs, and the following year Germany laid claim to what became called Tanganyika plus the provinces of Rwanda-Burundi. Britain retained "protectorship" over Zanzibar, while Germany became the ruler of German East Africa.

GERMAN EAST AFRICA

Tanganyika as a defined area did not exist before the Germans drew borders and it was marked on printed maps as German East Africa—it remained so from 1890 to 1918. Dr. Peters was the first governor. These were not happy times to start with. There was a series of natural disasters

KING MKWAWA AND THE GERMANS

One uprising against the Germans was led by King Mkwawa of the Hehe who refused to accept the German administration. He prevented their caravans from passing through what he considered Hehe land (near Iringa). In 1891 he ambushed a German patrol, killing hundreds of troops and capturing their weapons. The German response was strong and brutal. They lined up a battery of cannons against Mkwawa, who fled, and after four years of guerrilla war he shot himself rather than face capture.

accompanied by harsh rule by the Germans. Resistance to German rule led to several local uprisings. The Maji-Maji rebellion in 1905, in the southeast near Kilwa, was brutally crushed and a quarter of a million people died. Once heavily populated areas returned to bush and woodland.

At a cost of great human suffering, the local inhabitants gained themselves some improvements. Carl Peters was removed and his successor not only introduced laws to ensure better treatment of the local people but also encouraged their farming efforts so that they could make a profit growing cash crops. Their economy and living conditions were improving when World War I began in 1914. Africans were forced into a war in Tanganyika which was not their concern. Many never returned to their homes: some died of fever, some of hunger, and others were shot during the fighting. Most of what had been achieved was destroyed. The British eventually gained the upper hand against the Germans.

The Askari monument in Dar es Salaam pays tribute to the many African troops who died during World War I. It has now come to symbolize the sacrifice made by all Africans in wars not of their own making.

BRITISH TANGANYIKA

Under a League of Nations (the forerunner to the United Nations) mandate, the overseas territories of defeated Germany were given to the nations winning World War I. Britain took responsibility for the part of German East Africa which was renamed Tanganyika. The British governed the country from 1918 to 1963. Their method of indirect rule meant that many of the local tribal and village customs were retained. After 1947 Tanganyika came under United Nations trusteeship and Britain was required to slowly build up the political life of Tanganyika and prepare it for eventual self-government.

The British initiated the Groundnut Scheme in 1947 and aimed to plant vast areas of southeast Tanganyika with the valuable peanuts. But local conditions were unsuitable and all the work came to nothing.

WORLD WAR II

Although part of World War I was fought on Tanganyika's soil, causing destruction and misery, World War II had very different effects. As the world outside blew itself apart, Tanganyika got on with the business of growing food. Anything available for export was sold at a high profit. The country's export income in 1949 was six times higher than it had been when the war began. Even more important was the way that the people thought about themselves. About 100,000 joined the Allied

REVOLUTION ON ZANZIBAR

Zanzibar had become a British protectorate in 1890 and the islanders enjoyed many years of peace and prosperity. Even two World Wars did not disturb the island. The island achieved independence in December 1963. Peace was overturned a month later, however, when a revolution rejected the last of the Zanzibari sultans and the black African population waged bloody retribution on the Arabs for years of ill-treatment.

forces and fought on the side of democracy and freedom. When they returned home, they were determined that their own country would shake off its overlords and become a true independent democracy.

The Uhuru monument is dedicated to the freedom that finally came with independence in 1961.

TOWARD INDEPENDENCE

In gradual preparation for independence, in 1945, Britain appointed the first two African members to the Legislative Council. The movement towards independence gained strength after Julius Nyerere became the leader of the Tanganyika African Association (TAA) in 1953. By 1954 he had formed the Tanganyika African National Union (TANU), with the rallying slogan of *Uhuru na Umoja* (Freedom and Unity). After the first general election in 1958 three of the twelve cabinet ministers were African, and the growing support for TANU was clear. Even successful Asian and European candidates were those supported by TANU. In the 1960 election TANU triumphed and independence was only a year away.

NYERERE'S TANZANIA

Tanganyika became independent on December 9, 1961. The newly independent country was steered, created, and dominated by Julius Nyerere, one of the great statesmen of Africa. His TANU party won in the first round of elections and then formed Tanganyika's first government in December 1961. Nyerere's task was to rescue a country suffering from poverty and lack of economic structure. In April 1964 Zanzibar and Tanganyika joined to form the United Republic of Tanzania.

There were few challenges to Nyerere's authority, particularly after he made TANU the country's only legal political party. He was highly respected in world diplomatic circles and his opinions were respected since he continued to preach his doctrine of hard work as the answer to economic ills. He stepped down as president in 1985 but continued as chairman of the ruling political party until 1990.

During the Nyerere years (1964–85) Tanzania stayed safe from such horrors as military coups or civil wars even if Nyerere's socialism did not bring the economic

THE ARUSHA DECLARATION

In 1967, in what is known as the Arusha Declaration, Nyerere set out his ideals for African socialism and rural development. Since communities were so scattered, he developed *ujamaa* ("oo-JAH-mah"), the policy of familyhood, with a target of creating interactive communities and collective farms. At first it seemed to work, so in 1975 those who had not yet formed villages were forced to do so. But a lack of enthusiasm from people and poor management resulted in the failure of his collective farms.

success he had hoped for. Tanzania remained one of the world's poorest countries. Salaries of upper level government officials, including the president's, were cut harshly in 1966. Nyerere frequently reminded his people that they needed to work hard and be self-reliant.

WAR WITH UGANDA

The East African Community of Tanzania, Kenya, and Uganda was formed in 1967 with the aim of promoting trade and improving travel and rail links among the three countries. The organization collapsed by 1977—socialist ideas from Tanzania and capitalist ones from Kenya did not mix well. Nyerere closed Tanzania's border with Kenya in 1976. In addition, he refused to sit at the same table as Idi Amin, the leader of Uganda. By 1979 Tanzania was at war with Uganda, a response to troops sent by Idi Amin to northern Tanzania in the Lake Victoria region. Tanzanian soldiers forced the troops out and then advanced into Uganda. Amin was deposed and peace restored, but the financial cost to Tanzania was high.

Above: **Tanzanian troops remained in Uganda until they had overseen the election of Milton Obote.**

Opposite: **Julius Nyerere, president until 1985. He is often known as** *Mwalimu*, **the Kiswahili word for "teacher," and occasionally as** *yule Baba yetu*, **meaning "that father of ours."**

GOVERNMENT

WHEN THE TANGANYIKA AFRICAN NATIONAL UNION (TANU) WAS FOUNDED IN 1954, Julius Nyerere and the other planners aimed at making Tanganyika self-governing. They succeeded in seven years, and on December 9, 1961, their country became independent and a member of the British Commonwealth. Julius Nyerere guided Tanganyika at first as prime minister, then as president. With a reputation for moderation, TANU gained the confidence of non-Africans, and Tanganyika, later as Tanzania, gradually took a leading role in African politics.

Having rid themselves of colonial rule, the people wanted to rule themselves independently for the good of their own nation. Julius Nyerere led them in the path of socialism (working for the good of their community and country) rather than communism (everything being state owned and state controlled). Tanzanians were taught to be suspicious of the "greed of capitalism." Nyerere's "African socialism" may have helped to unite a varied population but it was a disaster financially.

Union with Zanzibar formed the United Republic of Tanzania, born on April 26, 1964. For a while there were regular elections but with only one party—and one candidate for president. Newspapers were tightly controlled. For a while only TANU party members were allowed to sell livestock in the market or to brew *pombe* ("POM-beh"), the moneymaking local beer. Disagreement with the government was considered a crime, and for a while Tanzania imprisoned political dissenters as freely as the South African regime that Nyerere denounced so vigorously. Now, however, there are several political parties and people are participating more freely.

Above: **Benjamin Mkapa was elected president of Tanzania in 1995. He served as foreign minister under Nyerere's leadership.**

Opposite: **Government building in Zanzibar.**

33

Village official addressing a gathering of people.

JULIUS NYERERE'S IDEALS AND THEIR FAILURE

Nyerere knew that in traditional African society everybody was a worker. This ideal was expressed in the Arusha Declaration of 1967. The scattered rural population was supposed to join together in the collective effort of *ujamaa*, familyhood communities, to increase output using large-scale agriculture and to provide social services such as water, electricity, and clinics. Many people were unwilling to move into these collective villages but were finally forced into them. They found that there was more opportunity for profit in the urban areas. The high ideals expressed by Nyerere, the "equality of man regardless of creed or color," were not always observed. Political leaders were not supposed to have private incomes, but did. Estates previously owned by whites or by Asians were confiscated to turn them into cooperative farms.

In the late 1970s the lack of financial success of the *ujamaa* villages, combined with drought, forced Nyerere to seek foreign aid. Reelected president in 1980 (again as the sole candidate), Nyerere announced that he would retire at the end of his five-year term of office.

GOVERNMENT ON ZANZIBAR

Liberated from its British protectorate, Zanzibar joined the United Nations in December 1963, and for 20 glorious weeks it was truly independent. Then an anti-Arab revolt deposed the sultan, and President Abeid Karume agreed to Zanzibar's union with Tanganyika to form Tanzania. The self-governance promised under this union never arrived. Even though the harsh rule of Karume ended with his assassination in 1972, Zanzibar was then under the control of the main political party of the new union. To voice disagreement was treason, and the island's main torture center became too well known.

Zanzibar has its own president. It also has its own Assembly and ministries. In 1993 Zanzibar's government arranged for the island to join the Organization of the Islamic Conference. But since they had not consulted the union government, this was declared unconstitutional. The economic strength of Zanzibar compared to the increasing poverty of mainland Tanzania has maintained an unspoken desire for independence. Zanzibaris fear that their island will be swallowed by the mainland. They have their own history, and they want Zanzibar once again to be a country in its own right.

The national flag combines the old Tanganyika and Zanzibar flag colors. Green is for the land, gold for mineral wealth, black for the people, and blue for the sea.

Government buildings in Zanzibar.

Party flags of the Civil United Front (CUF), a major opposition party in Zanzibar.

POLITICAL PARTIES

In 1977 TANU joined the Afro-Shirazi Party, which had been Zanzibar's only legal party, to form Chama Cha Mapinduzi (CCM, the Party for the Revolution). This was the only political party permitted in Tanzania until 1992, when President Mwinyi and the CCM leadership agreed to amend the constitution. The new bill allowed multiple parties, with the condition that parties must not be formed on tribal or racial grounds. The first multiparty election was held in 1995 with the following parties offering candidates: the CCM, the Party for Democracy and Progress (CHADEMA), the Civil United Front (CUF), the National Convention for Construction and Reform (NCCR-Mageuzi), and the Movement for a Democratic Alternative (MDA) of Zanzibar. The CCM was eventually declared to have won a majority in the National Assembly. The leader of the NCCR-Mageuzi, Augustine Mrema, has recently defeated the CCM candidate in an election in Dar es Salaam, which seems to indicate that his party may be the strongest opposition to the long-established CCM.

Former President Ali Hassan Mwinyi and his wife. Mwinyi was president of Zanzibar and vice-president of Tanzania before taking on his new office.

PRESIDENTS MWINYI AND MKAPA

President Ali Hassan Mwinyi took office in 1985. He met the worsening economic problems in the country by giving more encouragement to private businesses and accepting the International Monetary Fund (IMF) proposals on budgeting and agricultural reform. Foreign aid began to arrive as Mwinyi reassured investors and dismissed ministers who had opposed his economic plans. Later, Mwinyi too was accused of corruption and a Code of Ethics was introduced. Mwinyi was reelected as the only candidate in 1990.

In 1994 a corrupt scheme for avoiding as much as $70 million a year in import tax was uncovered. The IMF promptly froze all aid to Tanzania until 1996. Meanwhile the first election without a one-party system had occurred, in October 1995, although there had been some cries of vote-rigging in Zanzibar and elsewhere. In June 1996 Mwinyi stepped down as national chairman of the political party, CCM, and Benjamin Mkapa was chosen in his place. With the opposition parties split in their votes, Mkapa was then elected president of Tanzania with the backing of Nyerere, who vouched for his honesty.

Students at the CCM college near Dar es Salaam.

PARLIAMENT

The constitution of Tanzania establishes the offices of a president and two vice-presidents. The original intention was that one vice-president would be the prime minister and the other would be the president of Zanzibar. However, the constitution has been amended so that the president of Zanzibar is one of the council of ministers rather than vice-president.

The National Assembly of 244 members is formed by a complex formula including directly elected members from the mainland and Zanzibar as well as allocated seats for women, for members appointed by the National Assembly and by the president, and for appointed regional commissioners. Zanzibar has almost a third of the seats in the Assembly, although its population is less than 5% of the total.

A general election must be held at least every five years. Under the revised constitution, a president may not serve more than two five-year terms of office. The United Republic of Tanzania has 25 administrative regions: 20 on the mainland, three on Zanzibar, and two on Pemba.

JUSTICE

There is an independent judiciary with a four-level system of primary courts, district magistrates' courts, the High Court, and the Court of Appeal. The Chief Justice is head of the Court of Appeal, in Dar es Salaam. Zanzibar also has its own courts and the highest judicial authority there is the Supreme Council. The legal system includes English, Islamic, and customary law. The courts often deal with matters of traditional custom. There was, for example, a husband who demanded a refund of cattle from his bride price because his wife had given birth to only one child, but the case was settled in favor of the bride's parents. Recent legislation has given women more opportunity to seek justice.

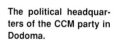

The political headquarters of the CCM party in Dodoma.

DODOMA

Although most of the government administration is based in the largest city, Dar es Salaam, Dodoma was chosen as the future national capital in an attempt to decentralize. It has a population of about 100,000 today. It was a small trading center for many years with caravan traders passing through. It grew in importance when the Germans decided to put the Central Railway line, which runs from Dar es Salaam to Kigoma, through Dodoma.

On the map Dodoma appears conveniently central, a stopping point on the east–west railway and on a north–south road, and with an airport. However, it is an unattractive place to live, is fairly dry and windy, and has a limited water supply. So far only the party political headquarters of the CCM has moved there.

Justice today is a welcome improvement from justice a hundred years ago when criminals on Zanzibar were still publicly beheaded by the sword.

FOREIGN POLICY

Tanzania is a member of the United Nations and of the Organization of African Unity (OAU), which was founded in 1963. It is also a member of the Southern African Development Community (SADC), which is interested in a more integrated common market among its member countries. Tanzania's Salim Ahmed Salim is the present secretary-general of the OAU.

Despite Nyerere's stated ideals of African unity, he believed it the duty of African leaders to intervene when neighboring countries were heading in a wrong direction. He helped topple three neighboring governments: in the Comoros in 1975, the Seychelles in 1977, and Uganda in 1978–79. Some 60,000 Tanzanian troops formed an "army of liberation" and joined Ugandan opposition forces that supported Milton Obote to defeat the brutal dictator Idi Amin and his Libyan allies in 1979. However, the Organization of African Unity condemned Tanzania's action as "interference in the affairs of a member state." Tanzania also had to pay the costs of the expedition alone—a bill of over $500 million. In November 1993 the presidents of Tanzania, Uganda, and Kenya signed a protocol on renewed cooperation among their countries.

DEFENSE

Tanzanian troops are used mainly to enforce law and order, but they saw active service in the war against Uganda. Many are on patrol in the troubled border region around the Great Lakes. There is compulsory service for two years; this may include working on civil works projects.

The army of about 30,000 is backed by a Citizens' Militia of around 100,000. There are eight infantry brigades and one of tanks, together with two each of artillery, anti-aircraft, mortar, and anti-tank brigades. The navy

of about 1,000 has patrol craft based on Zanzibar as well as on Lake Victoria. The Tanzanian air force was built up initially with help from Canada, with combat equipment that has been purchased from China. The air force has around 3,600 men.

Mounted police in Dar es Salaam.

AND TODAY?

The growing public awareness and outrage over corruption in the national leadership seems to point the way to a government increasingly willing to live by its ideals. Two finance ministers have been forced to resign in connection with schemes for avoiding import tax. The recently introduced Code of Ethics allows for investigations against accused politicians and civil servants. Although strong in neither economy nor military power, Tanzania is at peace and increasingly respected in African politics.

ECONOMY

NEVER A RICH COUNTRY in the days of German or British colonialism, Tanzania plunged into economic disaster in the 1970s, climbed out of trouble with huge injections of foreign aid, yet still ranks among the poorest countries of the world. Nevertheless, in African terms, it is still a paradise compared to Madagascar or the Democratic Republic of Congo. Sisal, cloves, and coffee form the principal export products; there is limited industrial activity and a slowly growing tourist income.

Most Tanzanians exist on what they can produce for themselves—in other words, subsistence living. Agricultural exports, such as tea, cloves, and cashew nuts, could prosper if world demand becomes sufficient. There are also mineral resources (diamonds, gold, gypsum), though in limited quantities, and increasing opportunities for tourism. But it is basically a poor country.

Above: **Fishermen on the coast of Zanzibar.**

Opposite: **Loading copper at Dar es Salaam's busy harbor.**

THE ROUTE TO DISASTER

President Nyerere, through his ideas on communal *ujamaa* villages, concentrated on the uplift of ordinary people struggling to survive in the widespread rural areas of Tanzania. Banks, hotels, and large businesses were to be nationalized and run by the state for the good of the whole country. His plan did not work, largely because of poor management and corruption. Many people lost the incentive to succeed— as anyone earning a high salary was taxed at the rate of 95% of their income, what was the point of working hard? In addition, world oil prices escalated, the East African Economic Community collapsed, and Tanzania spent a fortune on the invasion of Uganda. By the late 1980s, Tanzania was one of the largest recipients of financial aid in the world.

AGRICULTURE

There was a time when the soil of Tanzania was fertile enough to produce regular small crops to feed the scattered small communities. Then came *ujamaa*, which gathered people together in larger communities with the need for more concentrated farming of the land. This was followed by plantations and cash crop farming. Today some 80% of the workforce is engaged in agriculture, with the majority being women, yet agriculture only contributes 5% of the Gross Domestic Product (GDP) of Tanzania.

Much of the more systematic and successful agriculture was started by the German settlers who researched cultivation methods. They found a means of controlling the tsetse fly that was preventing human settlement in many infested areas. They introduced sisal, cotton, coffee, and tea.

Women winnowing rice, one of the main food crops. The rice is tossed into the air for the wind to separate the husk from the grain.

Children weaving palm leaf matting.

Only one-tenth of the land is suitable for farming because of poor soil and little rainfall. Most of the agriculture is subsistence farming (that is, providing food for home consumption) and is the only source of food for the 12 million people who live on maize, sorghum, millet, rice, peas, beans, and other vegetables. Yet agricultural products are also Tanzania's main exports, supplying around 80% of all exports.

Coffee, cotton, and tea are the most important cash crops. The reduction of state interference in rural marketing has encouraged more farmers to grow cash crops for local sale. Sisal is also a major cash crop. The leaves produce a hairy white fiber from which rope, string, and coarse mats are made. The port of Tanga depends on the sisal trade, and the country inland from there is covered with huge rectangular plantations. It is exported mostly in raw form, since Europe and other better-off countries put an extra import charge on rope, preventing Tanzania from making their own and selling it at a higher price. The use of synthetic fibers has reduced the call for sisal in recent years.

Children weaving palm leaf matting.

The World Bank has focused attention on flood control and irrigation as a means of adding 3.75 million acres (1.5 million hectares) to the country's farming land.

CLOVES

Tanzania is one of the world's main suppliers of cloves. Cloves were introduced to Zanzibar from Southeast Asia, probably from Indonesia, around the time of the first Arab sultan. Through the labor of slaves, Zanzibar quickly developed a flourishing trade in cloves. Although Zanzibar has been called "the island of cloves," a larger harvest comes now from the island of Pemba to its north. Many trees on Zanzibar were destroyed in an 1872 hurricane and Pemba took over as the largest producer. Many of these trees are owned by small-scale farmers and have been in the family for generations.

Everything about the clove tree is aromatic—leaves, flowers, and bark—but it is the sun-dried flower-buds that become the cloves to flavor food such as pumpkin pie. Oil of cloves is also used in perfumes and soaps. The unopened buds of the clove tree are picked and spread out on the ground to dry for about five days. When the cloves are being harvested, all schools close and everyone is there to help. With over three and a half million clove trees on Zanzibar Island alone, you can imagine the strongly scented air.

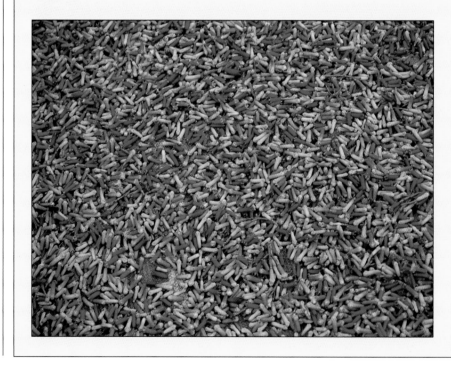

There are at least 6 million clove trees on the islands of Zanzibar and Pemba.

TRADE

As the majority of production is for home consumption, export trade is never high enough and vital imports often cost more than the country can afford. If the economy improves, Tanzania may attract foreign investors. The principal exports from the mainland are coffee, cotton, sisal, tea, tobacco, cashew nuts, diamonds, hides, and skins. From Zanzibar and Pemba come a large portion of the world's supply of cloves and clove oil.

The main imports are machinery, vehicles, industrial and consumer goods, building materials, fuels, metals, and chemicals. Dar es Salaam is by far the main port with several deep-water berths, a bulk-oil jetty, and a wharf for dhows and schooners. Some trade is also handled at Zanzibar, Tanga, and Mtwara, and at ports on the lakes. Uganda, which used to route most of its bulk trade through the Kenyan port of Mombasa, is now making greater use of Dar es Salaam. Bureaucracy and government inefficiency unfortunately do not make Tanzania a favored destination for traders.

A barge with trucks at Dar es Salaam harbor, the main port in Tanzania.

A clothing factory.

Tanzanite is a blue, semiprecious stone that comes from Tanzania.

MINING AND INDUSTRY

Mining has been dominated by the diamond mine at Mwadui, discovered by Dr. J.T. Williamson in 1940. On his death in 1958, all diamond shares were bought and divided equally between the Tanzanian government and De Beers Consolidated Mines. In that year diamonds ranked as the country's fourth leading export. Some gold has been mined near Lake Victoria, and prospectors have recently discovered fresh gold reefs in the district south of Lake Victoria. With the hope of extracting some 155 tons of gold, mining is due to start there in 1999. The Tanzanian government has a 15% stake in the project. Semiprecious stones (ruby, corundum, zircon, and amethyst) are available in small quantities, as well as tin and mica. Valuable deposits of coal and iron exist in the south, but their development as an asset is hampered by the poor access roads.

Nearly all manufacturing is the processing of agricultural products for sale within the country, including breweries and paper manufacture. Most electricity is produced from hydroelectric plants: much comes from the Pangani River, and there is potential power on the Rufiji. Machinery and spare parts are imported since Tanzania still lacks technical and design skills, and equipment is frequently abandoned because of local inability to repair it. Much of the foreign currency needed to acquire such imports comes from the tourism industry. Loans from the IMF are also helping provide the investment needed to develop industry within the country.

The oil company Engen has invested heavily in a bulk oil terminal in Tanzania, hoping to increase its operations in East Africa.

More than 300,000 tourists a year visit Tanzania. They come mainly to go on safari in the national parks or to climb Mount Kilimanjaro.

TOURISM

The government created the Tanzania Tourist Board to try and market the country's wildlife attractions together with focusing on environmental protection. Development in national parks is done in consultation with the World Conservation Union. The rewards for the economy are good: an attempt to climb Kilimanjaro will cost a visitor at least $500 with no guarantee he or she will get to the top! Big tourist companies whisk visitors around a safari circuit of Lake Manyara, the Ngorongoro Crater, Olduvai Gorge, and the Serengeti in a few days, although too many vehicles can raise dust clouds that affect good game viewing. If the road network could be improved, more visitors might discover the splendors of the Ruaha and Selous parks, as well as the almost untouched southern beaches. Marine tourism—for diving and fishing—is undeveloped so far.

Tanzania needs foreign exchange so badly that tourists are obliged to pay for almost everything in hard cash (US dollars or pounds sterling) and credit cards are seldom accepted. High taxes are imposed on tourists and the accommodation offered is not yet up to Western standards. Arusha has a conference center capable of accommodating 1,200 delegates.

Bus on a rift valley road.

TRANSPORTATION

Buses are the main means of transportation in Tanzania, though many roads are in terrible condition and not necessarily paved. They vary from usable to impassable. The Tanzam Highway was built as a joint venture between the Tanzanian and Zambian governments. Once known as "the hell run" but recently resurfaced, this road links the southwest of the country with Dar es Salaam. Roads in poorer districts are riddled with potholes and the traffic runs on whatever flattish surface is left. *Matatus* ("ma-TAH-toos"), the most heavily used buses, are usually crammed with people and their goods.

There are two railway systems: the Tazara line from Dar es Salaam to Zambia, and an older service, north to Moshi and west to Lakes Tanganyika and Victoria. The western line is the artery of Tanzania's heartland. Built by the Germans, it goes as straight as a highway across many miles of savannah plateau.

Dar es Salaam is the major port with three-fourths of all ships calling there. In the Indian Ocean, dhows and motorboats ply between coastal towns and islands, and there is a hydrofoil ferry service to Zanzibar. People who live near one of the Great Lakes travel by ferry to destinations along the shores. What may be the oldest steamer in regular service, the historic *MV Liemba*, has puffed up and down Lake Tanganyika since 1914.

Air Tanzania flies between Dar es Salaam, Zanzibar, Kilimanjaro, Kigoma, and Mwanza. A number of private airlines operate six- to eight-seaters. There are separate sets of fares for residents and nonresidents (who have to pay in US dollars). A number of international airlines fly to Dar es Salaam and a few touch down at Kilimanjaro and Zanzibar.

TODAY AND THE FUTURE

Much of Tanzania's tax money has to be used to pay interest on foreign aid or to pay state workers. It is difficult to develop much of an infrastructure as a result. In early 1997 another crippling drought occurred. The country's budget had to be revised for emergency spending for drought victims as some four million people faced food emergencies. The drought came at a time when burst pipes and poor organization was making water even harder to obtain. The nearly three million people who live in Dar es Salaam were particularly hard hit. Residents bought water by the bucketful from street vendors. There is talk of desalinating water from the Indian Ocean, but that is an expensive process and money is short.

Britain has released funds totalling $36.2 million to impoverished Tanzania. This is interpreted as a seal of approval on the new government of President Benjamin Mkapa. It seems that Tanzania is managing to maintain an image of what liberal-minded donors think an African country should be: socialistic, full of ideals, and sufficiently free from corruption.

Women at a well in the countryside.

"It is hard for a government to tell its people there is simply no cash."

—*Tanzanian finance minister*

51

TANZANIANS

GEOGRAPHY HAS ALWAYS INFLUENCED Tanzania's population. Those living on the inland plateau came from within Africa while settlers along the Indian Ocean coast came from outside. Several areas in the interior, with low rainfall and the tsetse fly, are sparsely populated. As a result two-thirds of the population lives only in the northern part of the country. Slave caravans in the past, raiding relentlessly into the interior, built up wealth and populations on the coast. Yet Tanzania is still one of the least urbanized countries in Africa with only 15% of the people living in towns.

Unlike many other African countries, Tanzania is not dominated by any one ethnic group. Although there is no warfare or striving for dominance among the tribal groups, there are struggles for power between Christians and Muslims. Tribes such as the Chaga and Haya which came under the influence of Christian missionaries in the colonial days now have a higher representation in the power structure than would seem appropriate to their numbers.

There are an estimated 120 different black African tribal groups. There are also small communities of Indian, Pakistani, European, and Arab people.

Left: **A tribesman with his goats.**

Opposite: **Masai women shave their heads and wear elaborate coils of beads on their necks and shoulders.**

Man and boy in Zanzibar.

THE MAIN ETHNIC GROUPS

SUKUMA The Sukuma live south of Lake Victoria and represent 15–20% of the population. Once fierce warriors who proved their manhood by spearing lions, they now live peaceably tending cattle and growing cotton, corn, and cassava in the fertile land around Mwanza.

MASAI These proud pastoralists live south and east of Lake Victoria, in nomadic style with precious herds of cattle. Often thought of as a Kenyan people, there are probably more Masai in Tanzania than in Kenya.

CHAGA On the slopes of Kilimanjaro, north of Masai country, live the enterprising Chaga. Their distinctive beehive-shaped thatched huts are fast disappearing, for the Chaga, a businesslike group, are finding increasing financial profit supplying guides and porters for tourists to Kilimanjaro. They also tend prosperous farms and coffee plantations on Kilimanjaro's fertile slopes.

SWAHILI *Waswahili* means "the coastal people," and because of their mixed African and Arab ancestry, the Swahili look more brownish gold than black, and their bone structure often shows a more European profile. Their language, Kiswahili, is now the national language.

GOGO Based around Dodoma, the Gogo tend herds and plant crops in a land desperate for water. Many still wear little but a flowing *kanga* cloth, with their earlobes bright with rings of copper wire. A hundred years ago they were strong enough to halt the advance of the Masai, but now their numbers are shrinking.

NYAMWEZI Their name means "people of the moon" and they were one of the most powerful tribes encountered by 19th century Western explorers. They live in the western savannah in and around Tabora.

HAYA Northwest of the Nyamwezi are the tea and coffee plantations of the Haya. Haya women produce excellent craftwork.

MAKONDE Famous for woodcarving, the Makonde live on a high inland plateau on the border with Mozambique. Regarded with a superstitious respect by nearby tribes, Makonde men file their teeth to sharp points and scarify their bodies in elaborate patterns.

HEHE Once feared and warlike, many of the Hehe now work as rangers and guides.

HA Living in a withdrawn forest world of mystic beliefs, the Ha are known for their marathon dance celebrations that may go on for several days and nights. They are cattle herders who still dress in natural materials.

"Hehe" is said to come from the battle cry "Hee-hee!" of the most famous Hehe chief, Mkwawa, who led years of resistance in the Iringa area against German colonizers.

NATIONAL CHARACTERISTICS

Some 60 million black Africans are sometimes referred to as Bantu, a name that also describes the related group of languages they speak. The word *bantu* means simply "the men" and is derived from *ntu* ("man") and given the plural prefix *ba*. Although mixed through the centuries with other peoples, such as Arabs, Persians, and Indians, most Tanzanians can be said to be of Bantu type, with dark brown skin (varying between black and tan), a broad face with high cheek bones, and a powerful, muscular physique. The Masai, however, are from the Nilotic group of tribes that originally migrated from north of Tanzania. The government discourages many tribal practices in order to build a sense of national identity, but the Masai retain many of their traditional customs. In character, Tanzanians are quick to smile and have an easy-going tolerance, but can be reserved in bestowing friendship.

The Tanzanians cling to their respect for authority. The president's picture is displayed in offices, restaurants, and schools everywhere— usually alongside a portrait of Julius Nyerere!

A crowd gathered in Zanzibar City.

REFUGEES

A recent influx of refugees is a problem for the Tanzanian government. In 1993 a failed coup attempt in Burundi (after the democratically elected Hutu government had taken office) sent a wave of refugees into Tanzania's Kigoma and Kagera regions in the northwest. More came after the outbreak of civil war in Rwanda in April 1994. There could be as many as 700,000 refugees in Tanzania, and the state of uncertainty in the Great Lakes region seems to indicate that there will be refugees in Tanzania for some time yet.

SEPARATE COMMUNITIES

In Dar es Salaam and along the coast where Africa is exposed to the ideas of the outside world more forcibly, there is frequent conflict between African Tanzanians and Asian Tanzanians. The Asians make up most of the merchant and business class and as such are often wealthier. The few wealthy Africans are primarily government officials, some of whom are suspected of being corrupt.

The various communities have their own customs. They may all drink together in bars and play games in teams together, but the racial communities tend to live apart and marry within their own community.

Girl wearing brightly colored *kanga*.

CLOTHING

Glossy brochures like to show Africans in traditional robes, beaded necklaces, and oversized earrings. The truth is that most Tanzanian men wear a T-shirt and jeans much like everybody else, often choosing bright colors. The richer businessman may favor an open-necked white shirt with a dark suit. Modern European-style clothing is seen by many as a sign of progress, sometimes as an indication that the family is now Christian. Even those wearing a traditional wrap draped over the shoulder will often have a modern dress or trousers underneath. Known as a *kanga* ("KAN-gah") on the coast, this wrap consists of a long straight length of brightly patterned cotton. This is cut in half; one half is wound around the body below the armpit and the other is draped over the shoulders or over the head by women. It is often worn over their other clothing. Poorer folk inland will keep a clean dress or *kanga* to wear to church or a party in the local beer club, while for the normal working day an old wrapper will do.

There are regional differences in clothing. In the predominantly Muslim areas along the east coast and on Zanzibar, the men wear the *kanzu* ("KAN-zoo"), an ankle-length white robe with a little fine embroidery at neck and hem, together with a red fez or a white embroidered Muslim cap. Some Muslim women wear a large piece of black calico (called a *bui-bui*) thrown over their heads like a hood, a requirement for modesty in Islam, but below this may be far more colorful clothing. In more traditional style, some women hide their faces from the sight of all men (other than a husband) apart from an eye-slit between headscarf and robe. Others, however, leave their faces uncovered.

Now that the days of Masai spears and Hehe muzzle-loaders are over, men carry a carved walking-stick, a long straight stick (useful for prodding cattle), or a rolled black umbrella.

THE MASAI

The Masai scorn modern styles and stand proudly in red blankets, their bodies and plaited hair smeared with red ochre and sheepfat. Men and women have elongated earlobes, hung with metal ornaments, and rows of beaded necklaces. Although the tall lion-spear is now forbidden, every Masai man carries a weapon of some sort. The young men go through a coming-of-age ceremony to become *moran* ("MO-RAHN") or warriors.

The Masai may not be typical of Tanzania as a whole, but they represent the pride of Africa with a continued refusal to be altered by Western civilization. Many of the other tribes have been encouraged to modernize their ways in the interests of national identity; the Masai have been allowed to continue their traditional lifestyle. According to their folklore, all the cattle in the world rightly belongs to them, since Ngai, their sole god, gave them to the Masai. So their duty was to protect the herds of their people and, logically, to capture other people's. Cattle represent the owner's wealth and so are very rarely killed.

Following the seasons, the Masai still remain an essentially nomadic people, moving over a great stretch of open dry country and frequently ignoring such modern impositions as national borders or the boundaries of game reserves. They are only slowly coming to accept changes in their lifestyle.

LIFESTYLE

BY WESTERN STANDARDS, Tanzania is a poor, struggling country where the majority of people live close to subsistence level. What money there is available seems to go to the few rather than to the many. Yet by African standards, rural Tanzanians are better off than those in many neighboring countries. There is a network of schools, health-care centers, and marketing cooperatives, even if supplies and standards are limited.

The countryside today is a mix of *ujamaa* communities, traditional isolated villages, state farms, and private estates. Many younger people are moving to the cities, though jobs there are few. For some families in the city, the children have to drop out of school to work so that there will be enough food. When people do manage to save enough money, they normally go home to the country where they buy land and houses. In this way they create security for their old age.

Where one all-embracing political party (the CCM) once ruled supreme, stifling any voice of protest, now there are new political parties with differing opinions. Education has brought awareness—of human rights, of gender equality, and of higher standards of living.

Left: **A busy bus stop.**

Opposite: **Swimming at the waterfront in old Stone Town, Zanzibar.**

Many of the young people are drifting toward the urban areas.

VILLAGE LIFE

Village life can be hard and a struggle to make ends meet. Most families live in one-story homes with corrugated iron roofs shaded by banana palms. If there is cash, the outside is painted. The women do most of the work, as well as bearing and bringing up the children. Women work the fields and prepare the food; men go fishing, tend cattle, work on a plantation, and build houses or fences. Most of every day is spent finding enough food to eat or water to drink. Without apparent effort, a woman will carry a heavy plastic water container or loaded woven basket on her head with a twisted cloth underneath for padding and balance. The children

THE MANY USES OF COCONUTS

The white meat inside coconuts is known as copra after it has been dried. Rope and string are made from the fibrous husk. But apart from these commercial uses, the coconut palm acts as a sort of department store for all. The nut provides a handy carryout meal and its juice a refreshing drink—quite alcoholic if allowed to ferment, when it is called *tembo*. Copra produces an oil that is used for cooking or hair care, or to make soap and candles. The dried fronds of the tree are used for thatching roofs and to weave mats, screens, and baskets. The attractively grained timber is used for ornaments. In all, the coconut is vital to the people of the coast.

On the rare evening for a party, benches are set out beneath banana trees and meat roasted on an open fire. The adults sit around drinking banana pombe *or European beer.*

work too. Girls guard the fields against birds and help their mothers in planting, washing, sweeping, and fetching water. Boys as young as 7 or 8 go out with their fathers, fishing or tending coconut trees or carrying tools.

If there is time for recreation, children play at being adults—the girls may play with sand, pretending they are pounding and cooking rice. They make up songs and dances, while the boys drum on a log. The first meal of the day is around 2 o'clock after the mother returns carrying water and wood (or bundles of thorns). In the afternoon the women are busy washing clothes, processing rice or cassava, and plaiting mats until after 8 o'clock, when prayers are said and the evening meal is eaten.

Above: **The Arusha Conference Center was built when Arusha was used as the capital for the East African Community. It has all the modern facilities including an interpretation system.**

Opposite: **Children often have to look after their younger siblings.**

URBAN LIFE

The urban population is growing at about 10% each year. Yet city jobs are so scarce that the government has been known to take truckloads of people, sometimes at gunpoint, back to the rural areas. Whether the people were being forced to live in *ujamaa* villages or merely being removed from overcrowded cities no one was sure. There is no such thing as unemployment benefits. People say *mnyonge hana haki* (a poor person has no right). Most try to sell something; this is called *mradi* ("mRAH-dee"), petty trade in handfuls of nuts, a fish, single cigarettes, or bundles of charcoal. Small-scale beer brewing creates quick money, though it is illegal.

Street kids and beggars live a desperate and degrading life. Boys called *wamachinga* ("WAH-mah-CHEEN-gah"), moving shopkeepers, who are usually migrants from rural areas, move around with heaps of items, such as kitchenware, clothes, and cosmetics, searching for customers.

Housing may also be hard to find and to afford. Many families live in a single room with a mattress on the floor as the only furniture, while those better off may have a small table and several wooden stools, several handwoven mats, and a number of beds and mattresses.

There are richer areas in all towns, of course. Well-fenced, spreading one-story villas (many of them built in earlier colonial days) form the residences of today's Tanzanian government officials, the wealthier businessmen, and the occasional foreign entrepreneur. An increasing number of German families, with ties perhaps from the days of German East Africa, are building homes along the coast.

BIRTH AND CHILDHOOD

Giving birth is the one activity where the men do not rule supreme. In rural tradition, a special hut was built where childbearing took place. In the town, the women of the extended family move in. The husband might visit but was not allowed in. If the mother was unable to breast-feed the baby, one of the other women would do so. Today's women do not want the large families of old, nor do their husbands. Children are expensive and, with modern medicine, more survive the birth process. The present birth rate is 4.5%.

In thousands of rural families it is still considered the duty of the eldest daughter to look after her younger brothers and sisters, while the eldest son will be the one who goes to school. More equal opportunities for boys and girls are slowly developing. The children are taught their social responsibilities by their family group as they grow up. In the rural areas many children still attend initiation school, but the circumcision that used to be part of the rite is no longer considered obligatory. While boys are taught a trade, girls often grow up taught that their objective is marriage. "A woman is incomplete without a husband," remains the belief for many.

MARRIAGE

An arranged marriage in which the girl has little or no say is customary for many Tanzanian families. Parents start planning a daughter's future very early on, for the system of bride-wealth is still very much part of the social tradition. The old logic says: "My women look after my home, working and planting and cooking. So if a man wishes to take away one of my daughters, he must make up for my loss." Where once a future husband might arrange bride-wealth in local beer, goats, and cattle, nowadays he will probably pay part or all in cash, perhaps paid in installments. The younger the bride, the higher the price. "If she is very young and a virgin she is worth a lot of cows," is how they used to put it.

Marriage arrangements differ according to local custom. With the Nyamwezi people the hopeful husband would give something to the

Village children on Chole Island

father of the girl he wished to marry. If the father accepted the gift, then the bargaining for the bride-wealth would begin. Once the parents have agreed on a husband, no daughter can refuse. It would be an embarrassment to her family and the entire village. She can reject a proposal but only with her father's consent.

For some tribes there is usually a time, perhaps two months, before the wedding when the future husband and wife get used to living together. The time comes for the agreed bride-price to be paid. Every male member of the bride's family—uncles, grandfather, and brothers—will get a share. Female relatives, except for the mother and perhaps grandmother, do not get anything.

Then comes the wedding, following either Christian or Muslim custom. The bride is given presents, usually household items for the kitchen, clothes, or money. There may follow a period when the new wife lives with her in-laws, being welcomed and looked after tenderly, but eventually the day will come when the two start creating their own home. Perhaps, in the course of living together and having children, they may even come to love each other as well. Even if she is unhappy, the bride may not go to stay with her own parents; they must not be seen as contributing toward the failure of the marriage.

As more Tanzanians go to live in towns and more children receive an education, the old customs are becoming weakened or ignored.

THE ROLE OF WOMEN

The patriarchal father-to-son tradition of most of Africa has left its women invisible in Tanzania as well. The place of women, forever in the field or kitchen, is essential to the economy but has no apparent cash value. For years the majority of urban women have worked on such tasks as food preparation, housekeeping, beer brewing, and petty trade. Only a few have found careers in nursing, teaching, or secretarial work.

The custom of a prospective husband paying for his wife, the bride-wealth, has not ceased. It may seem close to an insult for a woman to be "sold," but it also brings her respect for it gives her a clear worth. In an attempt to regulate marriage, the 1971 Marriage Act was passed, but the topic of bride-wealth was avoided. The Marriage Act also tried to limit the physical punishment which a husband could inflict on his wife, but during

Women working as receptionists at Mount Meru hotel.

68

Women at the market.

the parliamentary debate one member of parliament protested, "Beating a wife is similar to providing maintenance to a car. It corrects the problem, at least for a time."

Increasing educational opportunities, however, is helping women realize and achieve their place in society. In the cities, in particular, more women tend to be educated and involved in a variety of activities. To counteract continuing prejudice, seats are reserved for women in the Tanzanian National Assembly.

Centuries of tradition will take a long time to disappear. Some men consider women in politics to be "too independent." In Africa, boys are given priority in such matters as food, education, and attention. They will become the men who will have to lead and care for households. Only recently have educated men started to look for educated wives.

HEALTH

There are troubling reports of children inhaling pesticides while they pick coffee. There are almost no controls on pesticide use in Tanzania.

East Africa is not one of the healthiest regions of the world. Malaria (which kills around a million people in Africa every year) is always a threat; bilharzia, picked up from minute waterborne worms, is commonly present in the waters of Lake Victoria and Lake Tanganyika; sleeping sickness from tsetse flies and river blindness abound as well. An inoculation program for children exists but does not reach enough of them. Meanwhile, the greatest danger to health is quite simply a lack of proper food. According to UNICEF half the children in the country are malnourished. Although Tanzania escaped the Central African famines for several years, 1997 has been a time of bad drought.

There is a network of village dispensaries and rural health centers where overworked staff often have only the simplest medical facilities. Hospitals exist only in the major towns. Statistics indicate around one qualified doctor to every 25,000 people. Life expectancy is about 50 years for men and 55 for women.

It should be remembered that many Tanzanians do not seek modern medical help. They have greater faith in herbal medicines and traditional healers. In addition, the power of advertising has resulted in speedy sales of what are promoted as "miracle drugs."

AIDS

AIDS has been spreading in many African countries. In some countries, over 10% of the population are thought to be HIV positive. The disease is highest in the urban areas but is now spreading into the countryside. In neighboring Kenya, over half the hospital beds are filled with people suffering from AIDS or related sicknesses. Tanzania is well aware of the danger and has embarked on an effective publicity campaign.

THE JOURNEY TOWARD EDUCATION

The people of Tanzania have long realized that reading and writing were the means of obtaining well-paid work. At the turn of this century all education for Africans was in the hands of missionaries, and many of Tanzania's private schools are still run by religious foundations. Primary education is free, but although supposedly compulsory, only half the children attend school. At home, educated members of the extended family are frequently responsible for the education of younger ones. The desire for education is more than the government can afford. Some classrooms stand empty of desks or books. Only about 5% of primary pupils go on for secondary schooling. Most of these are in the urban areas for in the country it seems more important to start working early. Only about 3,400 each year enroll in higher education at the University of Dar es Salaam or the Sokoine University of Agriculture, Morogoro.

Literacy campaigns have raised the level of adult literacy from 33% in 1967 to around 68%.

Teaching is in Kiswahili, but the government is trying to improve English standards for higher education. All secondary schools are also expected to include practical subjects such as agriculture or bricklaying.

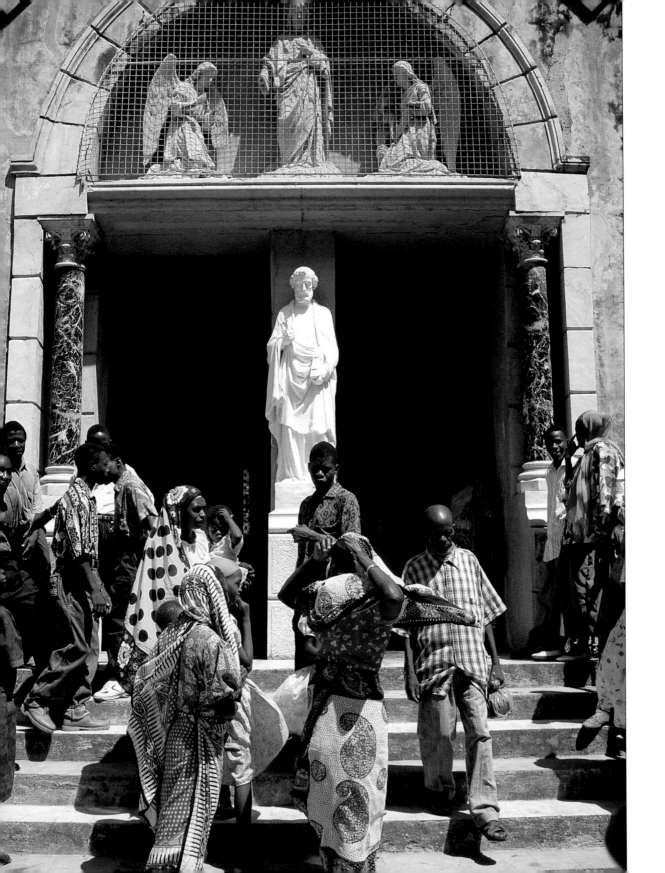

RELIGION

THE MAIN RELIGIONS in Tanzania are Christianity and Islam. The proportion is about 40% Christian and 35% Muslim, though these figures are misleading because many rural Tanzanians retain elements of traditional religions, while also practicing the Islamic or Christian faith. Others have not converted and stay firmly with their so-called "animist" beliefs. These include forms of ancestor worship and the belief that spirits exist in plants and animals or places such as volcanoes, mountains, or lakes. There are also small Asian communities of Hindus and Sikhs.

Many of the country's private schools and medical facilities are affiliated to mosques and churches. It is claimed that no religious bias exists in the country's political and civil administration, but certainly the feeling exists that those following traditional beliefs and not one of the accepted world religions are less civilized. Nevertheless, officially there is freedom of religious worship.

Left: **A Muslim girl in Stone Town, Zanzibar.**

Opposite: **Congregation leaving St. Joseph's Cathedral.**

ISLAM

The Arab word *islam* means to surrender to the will or law of God. Someone who surrenders his or her life to Islam is called a Muslim. For the millions of Muslims the world over, Mohammed is the Prophet of God (whom they call Allah) who brought the teaching of Islam to the world as written in the Koran.

This religion was brought to the east coast of Africa about seven hundred years before Christianity made any great impact. Tanzania's coastal towns were established by Arabs, therefore their inhabitants are predominantly Muslim. The islanders on Zanzibar are 96% Muslim

Below: **Many Muslim children are sent to Koranic schools in addition to their regular schooling.**

Opposite: **The main Ismaili Mosque is in Zanzibar.**

(the other 4% being Hindu) and the first mosque was built there in 1107. Since then around 50 other mosques have been built. Zanzibar also has Muslim courts that deal specifically with laws on marriage, divorce, and inheritance. In 1935 Sheikh Mubarah Ahmed was entrusted with the task of preparing a Kiswahili translation of the Koran from the original Arabic.

Most Muslims dress conservatively: men usually wear a black or white Muslim cap, while women drape their heads with a black veil. In addition to attending a regular school, the children go to Islamic school to learn the Koran in Arabic. They follow the Islamic calendar and observe Muslim festivals such as Eid el-Fitr.

Many of the Asian Muslims belong to the Ismaili sect under the spiritual leadership of the Aga Khan. After the end of World War I, Ismaili Muslims established schools, hospitals, dispensaries, and libraries in coastal areas of Tanzania. The Muslim Sunni and Shi'a sects are present in Tanzania as well. The different communities mostly keep to themselves, especially when it comes to marrying, though this is changing a little among the younger people.

A baptism in the river.

MISSIONS AND CHRISTIANITY

Because of the early establishment of Islam along the coast, Christianity in Tanzania had a greater influence inland. The country has some 8.4 million Christians (mostly Roman Catholics, with some Lutherans, Anglicans, and Presbyterians) compared to a total of around 9 million Muslims.

The earliest Christian missionaries in Tanzania came from the Church Missionary Society. Dr. J.L. Krapf set out from Zanzibar in 1844 with a letter of introduction from Sultan Sayyid Said to Arab governors: "This letter is written on behalf of Dr. Krapf, a good man who wishes to convert the world to God. Behave well to him, and be everywhere serviceable to him." The letter must have helped because Krapf, despite the death of his wife and child from malaria, laid the foundations for a number of mission stations.

The first Catholic mission established its base in Bagamoyo, where in 1868 the Fathers of the Society of the Holy Ghost built what is now known as the Fathers' House. As Christian missionary work moved inland, the

London Missionary Society purchased a steamer for work on Lake Tanganyika in 1876. In addition, responding to an appeal by David Livingstone, the Universities Mission to Central Africa set up its first mission station at Magila, in the hilly country behind Tanga. From here a number of other mission posts were opened, with schools and hospitals.

After losing their struggle against the colonizing Germans in 1905, many of the Tanzanian tribes abandoned the traditional spirits and magic that had failed to protect them. There were mass conversions to Christianity. The work of the Christian missions, with their churches, schools, and medical clinics, helped to establish the ideals of European civilization, though they were often insensitive about respecting local customs. They were regarded as subversive by some as they taught women new ideas about freedom, love, and marriage. One of the traditional customs halted by the arrival of Christianity was that of polygamy, a man having several wives. The Christian missions could not stop the way that parents chose husbands for their daughters, but they did allow boys and girls to meet more often in church and school.

A nun on the steps of a church.

THE MORAVIAN CHURCH

The work of the Moravian church was particularly significant in rural areas. The Moravians taught literacy alongside the Christian moral code. Their love of singing and church music made the Moravian missions highly popular and they continue to be centers of activity, often linking several villages together. Services are often colorful and noisy with an African band playing.

A traditional healer performs his own dance rituals.

Pemba is a popular center for African medicine. People needing to be cured of mental or bodily ailments come from Zanzibar and the mainland to visit Pemba's traditional doctors.

TRADITIONAL BELIEFS

The growing strength of Christianity and Islam has not stopped the many traditional beliefs that abound in Tanzanian society. Many people continue to hold their belief in spirits or witchcraft alongside their Islamic or Christian beliefs. For example, a string of selected leaves above a doorway is said to keep out evil spirits. Anyone foolish enough to pick one of the white flowers of the baobab tree is certain to be eaten by a lion. Red-rimmed eyes are said to be a clear sign of witchcraft. On Zanzibar, parents make sure their children behave by telling them scary tales of the *popobawa* ("poh-poh-BAH-wa"), which is supposed to be a cruel dwarf with one eye and bat-like wings. Many adults also claim to have bones broken by *popobawa* attacks in the night. After a disaster on Lake Victoria in which the ferry *MV Bukoba* capsized and sank, relatives of those drowned followed an ancient ritual. They wove a white shroud, weighted it with rocks and lowered it into the lake to pacify the watery spirits so that they would not claim others in the same way.

SHOEBOX LIBRARIES

This worthwhile project was launched in Dar es Salaam in 1968, copying the initiative of Joyce Chaplin, founding editor of Africa Christian Press in Ghana. Each cardboard box contains 20 booklets—10 in Kiswahili and 10 in English. The books are mainly Christian, but these mini-libraries also include books on topics such as health, nutrition, agriculture, literacy, or raising children. A small deposit is charged to ensure their return. In some areas a reading room is set up in a school or church and people can sit and read there without charge.

Project Habari in Moshi trains librarians and starts small rural libraries. Sponsored by the Evangelical Lutheran Church in Tanzania, some 50 parish librarians have been trained; their aim is that every congregation will have a library and a librarian.

At times, however, there may also be opposition to some Christian efforts. Hephzibah Hall, who runs a Christian bookshop in Moshi, says that people tell her, "Don't you know that Christianity is a white man's religion and they use it to oppress us? Why aren't you selling black books?" But she believes the books are glorifying God, and now people come to her shop to study and pray.

The method used in magistrates' courts of swearing on the Bible does not carry the same solemn constraint to tell the truth for traditional-minded Tanzanians as the old tribal oaths did. With the Chaga people, a man may gather a little soil from the ground, put it in his mouth and say, "If I lie let this earth kill me."

OL DOINYO LENGAI

The Masai consider the active volcano, Ol Doinyo Lengai in northern Tanzania to be the "Mountain of God." It is the sacred place of their god Ngai and of his messenger Kindong'oi, from whom they believe their priests are descended. If the peak is not in sight (due to the Masai moving around with their grazing herds), they will conduct their worship under specially designated fig trees. They pray, particularly at sunrise, for protection from natural evils such as drought and famine.

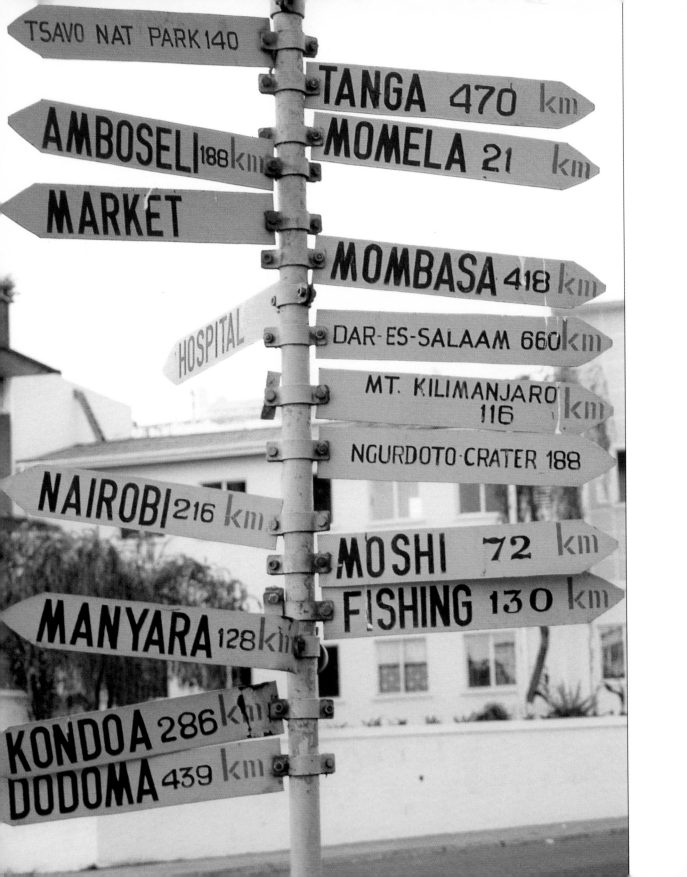

LANGUAGE

THE PROSPEROUS ADVANCEMENT of the Arab-dominated coastal regions resulted in Kiswahili ("ki-swah-HEE-lee") becoming the language used for commerce and government throughout the country. When the country was German East Africa, Kiswahili was used also as the language for government matters. Today Kiswahili is the country's official language, and although it is spoken as a mother tongue by only about 9% of the population, 90% of Tanzanians use it as a second language.

Some remote rural areas cling to their own dialects. Tanzania has some 120 different linguistic groups, all of which are confined to specific tribal areas. The Masai, for example, speak their own Masai language, which is totally unlike anything else spoken locally and is thought to belong to the Nilotic group of languages that originated in the Nile valley. Some English is spoken in the larger towns and popular tourist destinations, as well as being used for commerce and government.

Primary education is in Kiswahili, though the teenagers who go on to secondary school show an increasing desire to learn English as well.

Left: **Tanzania has several Kiswahili daily newspapers.**

Opposite: **Street signpost in Arusha.**

A sign in Arabic.

WHERE DOES THE LANGUAGE COME FROM?

There seem to be four main root languages in Africa, corresponding with geographical areas. The mother tongue of most Tanzanians comes from the Niger-Congo region of western Africa. This group of languages is often called *Bantu*, a word which means "the people," coming from *ntu* ("man") and the plural prefix *ba*. The Bantu languages were originally only *spoken* languages. The idea of having a written form of language was introduced to East Africa by foreigners—first the Arabs (who wrote Arabic) and later the European missionaries (who wanted to translate the Bible into the local language).

KISWAHILI IS BORN

The Arabic word *sawahili* means "of the coast" and was first used to describe the people that visiting Arab traders met there. By the 12th century, there was a tribe calling themselves the Swahili who built towns, forts, and palaces. The demands of trade required easy communication between the Arab traders and Africans, so the Bantu mother tongue spoken by the Swahili gained an added mixture of Arabic words. Attempts to capture the language in writing (at first using the Arabic script of the Koran) led to further changes in the language. Under British influence, Kiswahili changed a bit more as writers used the Roman alphabet (which we use for English). The first dictionary of Kiswahili was compiled in 1903.

Kiswahili was originally spoken only by the inhabitants of the east coast. It penetrated westward with the Arab ivory and slave caravans and is now the main language of Tanzania, Kenya, and Uganda, as well as being spoken in many parts of eastern and central Africa. Together with Hausa, it is one of the most widely spoken African languages. When you include all the Kiswahili-speaking communities around the world, the total comes to nearly 50 million people. Although there are several regional dialects, the purest Kiswahili is supposedly that spoken on Zanzibar, and the Institute of Kiswahili & Foreign Languages is on the island.

Most Tanzanians talk to each other in Kiswahili, largely as a result of the efforts of Julius Nyerere to be rid of the remnants of such colonial languages as German and English. For example, in 1974 Nyerere ordered that all titles in Tanzania, including "Mister" should be replaced by *Ndugu* ("un-DOO-goo") meaning "brother." By making Kiswahili the national language, Nyerere was also attempting to unify the country and create a sense of national identity larger than the many tribal identities.

Uhuru primary school. The medium of instruction in Tanzania's primary schools is Kiswahili.

THE NAME OF THE LANGUAGE

Although often referred to as Swahili, the correct name for the language is Kiswahili. The first syllable (prefix) of *ki* indicates that it is a language. English (in Kiswahili) is *Kiingereza* and French is *Kifaransa*. In the same way, the prefix *wa* indicates a group of people, so the speakers of Kiswahili are correctly known as Waswahili.

HOW DOES THE LANGUAGE FIT TOGETHER?

Our English language uses many suffixes, which are additions to the *end* of the word. To make a word plural we usually add the suffix "-s," for example turning "book" into "books." In Kiswahili, as with many of the Bantu languages, a prefix is added (at the *beginning* of the word) instead of a suffix. For example, the prefix *m* is singular and *wa* is plural. So *mtu* means "a person," while *watu* means "people." When a noun is linked with an adjective, both prefixes change: so, *mtu mzuri* means "a good person" while *watu wazuri* means "good people." (The "m" at the beginning of a word is pronounced like "hum" without the "hu.")

Here are a few common Swahili words:

hoteli ("ho-TELL-ee"): a local restaurant, not a hotel

banda ("BAN-dah"): a hut

aiskrimu ("ah-ees-KREE-moo"): ice-cream

mayai ("mah-YAH-ee"): eggs

wazungu ("wah-ZOON-goo"): white people

Kiswahili is Romanized, and children learn the rudiments of language using the alphabet that Western children know.

GREETINGS

Jambo ("YAM-boh") is the Kiswahili for "hello" and is used as a general greeting. The greetings *Hujambo* ("hu-YAM-boh") or *Habari* ("ha-BAR-ree") both mean "How are you?"

Many Africans have an elaborate ritual of greetings before they move on to any further conversation. When two men meet, after the initial *Jambo mzee*, there will be solemn enquiries about the other's health and his family, and only then *Habari gani?* ("hah-BAH-ree GAH-nee"), or What's new? *Mzee* ("m-ZEE") is a term of respect, particularly used by younger to older. Another more common term of respect (like sir or mister) is *bwana* ("BWAH-nah"), a short form which means "the father of many sons." To an older woman, one says *bibi* ("BEE-BEE"). In business or polite conversation, Tanzanians often address each other by their last name. They use first names only in their family.

In some parts of Tanzania it is considered polite to clap the palms of the hands together when thanking someone or greeting a person who has come from afar. This is also done when they are in mourning for someone's death. The threefold African handshake, using palm, thumb, palm, is also widely used. (But the thumb sign used by hitchhikers in some countries may be considered a rude gesture!)

If you are invited into someone's home, you will be greeted with Karibuni! ("ka-ree-BOO-nee")— Welcome!

Two women greeting each other with a clasp of the hands.

PUBLISHING

The oldest publishers in Tanzania were the missionary presses that printed Bibles and religious pamphlets. Then came the government printers, which from colonial times have produced copies of laws, the government gazette, and sometimes official newspapers. The government has also printed textbooks for secondary and advanced levels of education. There are also "parastatal" publishing houses such as Tanzania Publishing House, which are joint ventures between the government and overseas firms. Small, private publishers seldom survive unless they manage to get at least one book accepted as a school supplementary reader. Outside the educational field, books and publishing have been considered part of the struggle to "construct a socialist society" and break away from capitalism. In that form, publishing is thriving in Tanzania, though the publications are seldom known outside the urban areas.

It is hard to obtain many of the daily papers outside of Dar es Salaam.

Tanzanians do read books, it seems, but they seldom buy books. They connect books with education and therefore expect the books to be provided by the school or college. Many also do not have the extra cash to spend on books, which are expensive and as a result are mostly a luxury item. There are few bookshops in Dar es Salaam, apart from some second-hand book stalls and kiosks where international news magazines are popular. There are not many libraries either, although the island of Pemba proudly opened its first ever public library in 1994. It now has 1,500 regular users, mostly from Chake Chake (Pemba's main town), with a book stock of about 13,000 titles.

The radio is the main source of news in rural areas of Tanzania.

THE MEDIA

The news media have been carefully controlled by the government for many years. President Nyerere stated quite openly, "No government likes to be criticized," which was why the main newspapers belonged for a while either to the government or to the main political party. However, in recent years, privately owned newspapers in both English and Kiswahili have appeared. Kenyan newspapers are also available in Tanzania.

Tanzania runs a state-controlled radio with programs in Kiswahili and English. Television news is in Kiswahili. In rural areas with no newspapers, the people rely on radio broadcasts for their news. The government has also used radio programs to promote adult literacy and to spread information on better nutrition and ecological conservation.

Tanzanian children's literature also includes books from abroad. Roald Dahl's popular Charlie and the Chocolate Factory *has been translated into Kiswahili.*

THE CHILDREN'S BOOK PROJECT

This project was started in 1991 in response to the acute shortage of books in Tanzania, especially books for children. Supported by international donor organizations in Denmark, the Netherlands, Canada, and the Aga Khan Foundation, the project produces children's books in Kiswahili. These books are distributed to rural libraries, primary schools, and teachers' centers, and some are sold to bookshops. By September 1994, a total of 60 books had been produced and another 45 were in production. The project also runs courses for writers, publishers, and illustrators.

ARTS

THE IDEA OF AN "ARTIST" was almost unknown to early African people. The ancient painters who created the paintings of dancers, giraffes, and buffalo on huge boulders near Dodoma were probably thought of as priests or medicine men in their hunter-gatherer culture. These paintings are the oldest indigenous art in Tanzania. The painter or the carver in Africa was not an individual creating a work of art for personal satisfaction. He or she was merely one of the community who happened to be better at painting or carving than the others, someone who created what was required by the community, yet always with a touch of individuality. African sculpture is closely connected with traditional beliefs in the spirits of ancestors and the conviction that the course of events can be influenced by magical practices.

Alongside traditional art of the African tribes other artistic styles also occur in Tanzania due to the influence of early Arab and Indian traders. These are reflected particularly in the architecture on the east coast.

Today, among Tanzania's noted artists are Francis Msangi, who makes delicate lino prints, and Sam Ntiro, who does African religious scenes.

Left: **A batik painting with many of the animals of the safari.**

Opposite: **Zanzibar is known for its beautifully carved doors.**

CARVING AND CRAFTWORK

African woodcarvers seldom waste wood on an item with no practical use. Yet they also lavish great skill on their craft items. A village elder will have a more elaborately carved stool than the plain ones used by many women. A typical traditional throne for a Nyamwezi chief might have a three-legged circular seat with a tall curved backrest, carved with a suitably imposing human figure. Neck supports and combs were important to allow a person to sleep without disarranging the hair, for in such tribes as the Masai the men spend an enormous amount of time arranging their hair and headdress. Arab chests from Zanzibar with elaborately carved detail indicate the wealth that might be locked inside.

Masks were created for specific dances on occasions such as the initiation into adult life or a ritual to bring rain or increase crops. For these, the carved faces might represent dead ancestors or their spirits. Others were carved to scare away evil spirits or to increase fertility so that the tribe became numerous and strong.

MAKONDE

The story goes that the first carver lived alone in the forest. There he shaped a piece of wood into a female likeness and left it outside his hut overnight. In the morning he found the carving had come alive and was now a beautiful woman. Their child was the first true Makonde.

Perhaps the most famous wood sculptors in Africa, the Makonde have been carving for at least 300 years. They came originally from northern Mozambique and now live in the southeast part of Tanzania, on the relatively isolated Makonde Plateau. They have built villages of woodcarving workshops, where they sell their crafts to tourists or curio dealers. They carve face masks, figures, and drums. They carve ghosts and spirits from the legends of their people. The human faces that they carve are gaunt, grotesque, and intricately decorated with geometrical tattooing. Male masks are bearded, sometimes with human hair; female masks always have a disc-shaped peg set in the upper lip. Modern styles have become more imaginative and abstract. Some called *Sheteni* ("SHEH-ten-ee"), portray devilish figures and flesh-eating monsters based on Makonde folklore.

DAILY ITEMS

Whether the countless objects made for everyday use—baskets, pottery, mats, metalwork, jewels, beads—are classed as craftwork or art is debatable. Most are made to earn some quick cash; a few are made with style and skill. Beads are used extensively by Tanzanians for bodily adornment. Originally they were made from ostrich egg shell. Then came imported glass or ceramic beads, but the skill of arranging them and the distinctive patterns are African. Other handicraft include mats or baskets woven from young palm fronds or dried banana leaves. Pots are both decorative in the home and useful, since many Tanzanian housewives prefer to cook in clay pots rather than metal ones.

LITERATURE

The oral (spoken) literature of East Africa is endless and includes proverbs and riddles, myths and legends, and interwoven songs and dances. Storytelling remains a skill of which many Tanzanian mothers are proud—and which has not been lost to television since television has not reached much of Tanzania.

The first-known written work in the Tanzanian region, written about 1520, was in

Arabic and was the history of the city-state of Kilwa Kisiwani. This was followed by histories of other cities written in an early form of Kiswahili. In 1728 the epic Kiswahili poem *Utendi wa Tambuka* (Story of Tambuka) inspired a steady stream of story verse with Arab themes romantically flavored for East African readers. A Kiswahili novel by James Mbotela, *Uhuru wa Watumwa* (Freedom of the Slaves) was published in 1934, but it was the writing of the Tanzanian poet Shaaban Robert in the 1950s and 1960s that gained genuine respect for Kiswahili literature.

President Julius Nyerere was a respected author and translator. His work *Education for Self-Reliance* set out his theories on a suitable education system. Appreciative of culture, he also translated two of Shakespeare's plays into Kiswahili—*Julius Caesar* and *The Merchant of Venice* (which, in his translation, he called "The Capitalist of Venice").

Opposite: **Woman weaving baskets.**

One of the legends told is of Mount Kilimanjaro and relates that the treasured jewels of King Menelik I of Ethiopia, son of Sheba and Solomon, are buried under the peak, Kibo. Anyone finding the ring of Solomon among these jewels will be endowed with his wisdom.

LITTLE GRANNY

Fatuma Bintibaraka from Zanzibar is known affectionately as "Little Granny" (she is over 80). For many years, in the 1920s and 1930s, the Zanzibaris heard her lilting voice but never saw her face, for Islamic women were required to cover themselves from head to toe when in public. She learned all her songs from Siti Bintisaad, the first woman singer in Zanzibar, and she sings in Arabic and Kiswahili for she speaks no English.

Fatuma became famous outside Tanzania, and in the 1980s she toured Germany, Japan, the Gulf, Paris, and London with a *taarab* ("TAH-rab") band which plays traditional music from Egypt using fiddles, flutes, drums, and rattles. Now she has discarded her veil and drinks beer and smokes. She plays with the Shikamoo Jazz Band, veteran musicians raising money for the aged in Tanzania. This is her personal *uhuru*, an adventurous journey of freedom.

Village *ngomas* ("un-GOH-mahs") or dances are held for many different occasions.

MUSIC AND DANCING

In his first year as president, Julius Nyerere set up a Ministry of National Culture to encourage a wider appreciation of indigenous art forms. He was particularly concerned that traditional dancing was being forgotten. He said, "How many of us can dance, or have even heard of, the *gombe sugu*, the *mangala*, the *konge*, or the *lele mama?*"—all names of Tanzanian dances. In due course, university students were ordered to take traditional dance classes, and Tanzania's newly formed National Dancing Troupe soon toured the country, learning and performing dances from all the regions.

Music and dance are part of the same process, for the musician moves his body and limbs during the process of making music. (It is virtually impossible to capture true African music in musical notation on paper.) Sometimes everybody present takes part; sometimes musical specialists lead the music or dance pattern or perform on their own. Many traditional dances feature masked dancers, often performing in pairs. The masks may represent animals or devil spirits or ancestral spirit powers. Dancers may also use body paint or costumes, rattling gourds and strings of beads, and they may hold spears or marimbas. Singing is a way of communicating and very often songs have a "call and response" pattern. In the same way that words in African dialects can change meaning according to the intonation and pitch of the voice, so sung music tends to follow the setting and rhythm of the words.

Drumming, dancing, and songs are often part of special ceremonies. They may celebrate the initiation of youths who have been accepted as men, try to please the spirits of the ancestors, or try to drive away evil spirits that might affect the fertility of the tribe or their cattle. Drums, which help hold a rhythm or build up tension, are nearly always used. There are many different types. Some are pointed at one end so that they can be firmly bedded in the ground, some have their own legs or supports, and some are held between the knees.

A Makonde man playing a tambusa drum.

Another percussion instrument is the xylophone, which makes use of the resonant qualities of different woods. Hand-clapping and foot-stamping is also popular. Tanzanian music also uses string instruments with resonators (such as a coconut shell or gourd) and pipes made of bamboo or animal horns.

All these instruments have their root in traditional music, but they are also used to create modern swing and jive music. In addition, what might once have been solemn chanting and hymns sung in local churches have instead been greatly livened up by the pleasure many Tanzanians take in choral singing.

ARCHITECTURE

There is no memorable style of house peculiar to Tanzania, probably because of a lack of permanent materials, combined with the nomadic or small-settlement quality of so much of the lifestyle. The use of natural materials (wood, mud, twigs, thatch) results in impermanent structures that soon rot in the heat and humidity. Poles from mangrove trees are still used for building because the wood is resistant to termites. The more permanent architectural styles in Tanzania arrived with settlers or colonizers: Islamic mosques, Indian carved doors, Bavarian buildings, and British colonial hotels in Dar es Salaam, and more recently, uninspired modern apartment and office blocks.

A viilage house made of mud and poles.

On the island of Zanzibar, however, buildings have a particularly distinctive feature. It became the custom to build the doorway of a house before the house itself—as the entrance, it was considered to be key to the well-being of the building. Square frames of solid teak were installed, often with decoratively carved Koranic (Islamic) texts, believed to increase the good fortune of those dwelling inside. Under later Indian influence, doors with arched tops and more elaborate designs were also introduced. Motifs with specific meanings were carved among geometric and floral designs: chains represented security, the precious frankincense tree stood for riches, shoals of fish encouraged fertility, and the sacred lotus was a symbol of reproductive power.

Sadly, the historic buildings of Zanzibar have suffered from neglect and decay. So it is heartening to see such benefactors as the Aga Khan (spiritual leader of the Ismaili Muslims) sponsoring restoration, while a number of other buildings are being preserved by selling them to private owners.

The 1894 Old Dispensary in Zanzibar was restored by the Aga Khan Trust for Culture and now serves as the Stone Town Cultural Center.

The impressive "House of Wonders" Palace built for Sultan Barghash in 1883 preserves some of the most striking Zanzibar doors under the shade of its wide-spreading verandahs.

LEISURE

WHAT IS "LEISURE" when you work all day to grow enough food to survive? Perhaps it is listening to the radio when it is too dark to work any more. Or singing and worshiping and meeting friends at church on Sunday. Whether the reason is a joyous wedding or a sorrowful funeral, a gathering of the extended family is given high priority. People travel great distances for special occasions despite the problems of the Tanzanian transportation system.

Tanzanians love music and dancing, so the village *ngomas*, or dances for different social occasions, are welcomed by all. There may be a live band with some traditional dancing, or perhaps someone has a tape of a popular rock group. There are discos in most towns now as well as in villages, even if they play just scratchy disks on a battery-operated player. Movies are a favorite leisure activity. There are six cinemas in Dar es Salaam, and the popular taste is for action features involving war, gangsters, and kung-fu fighting.

Left: **Young Tanzanians.**

Opposite: **The streets of Zanzibar are busy with people at all hours.**

RELAXING

On most evenings the older folk will sit and talk, often the men and women sitting separately. In towns, the men will sit along a bar with a few bottles of Safari lager (unless they are Muslim); in the villages, there will be homemade beer under the spreading branches of a tree. If it is a hot night and the young ones cannot sleep, their grandmother may keep alive the old custom of storytelling with some folktale of giants, cannibals, or talking animals.

BAO

Bao ("BAH-oh") is a traditional African game (similar to *kigogo* played in Kenya) and uses a wooden board with parallel rows of holes, or just hollows scooped out of the sand. The two players have pieces (beans or pebbles) that they place in a way that will "capture" their opponent's pieces. The rules are complicated and tend to be different from place to place.

Young men and women are encouraged to socialize, in contrast to years gone by when they would have been lucky to meet briefly on the way home from church.

CHILDREN'S GAMES

Children play make-believe games in Tanzania, as they do anywhere. But they are also required to help with the domestic chores. Some help each other fetch water or weed vegetables, so that there is time for play at the end. The boys play war games, firing "bullets" of dried leaves with their catapults. The girls play "weddings," using dolls made from scraps of cloth and fiber with black thread for hair. "Bring the boy friends! Bring the money! For my child I want 200." So the bride-wealth is arranged and paid and perhaps a make-believe "cow" is killed for the feast. "Now let's have the wedding. There's a wedding today at my place!" With much drumming and dancing, the two dolls are placed side by side in bed!

Another favorite game is "The Monkey Game," much like hide-and-seek where one child is "it" and stays by the goal while the others run and hide. They call out, "Oh, ooh, ay!" and the one who is "it" goes to look for them. Any child touched and caught must go and wait by the goal (like a tied-up monkey) until all have been caught.

Young boys with home-made toy cars.

Children also play "The Blindfold Game" where all the children are covered up with a blanket except for one. That child has to feel the others through the blanket until she or he recognizes one and calls out the child's name.

SPORTS

Soccer is the great game everywhere, to play or to watch or to shout about. In the smallest villages boys will kick around a ball made of rags if they don't have a better one. Crowds will go to support their favorite local teams in the larger towns. The Zanzibar soccer team won the East and Central African Challenge Cup by beating Uganda 1-0 in the final on December 9, 1995. By way of reward, each player received a motorcycle as a present from Zanzibari President Salmin Amour. In addition, the goalie (Rifat Said) and the player who scored the winning goal (Victor Bambo) received one million Tanzanian shillings from the delighted president. This was the first time Zanzibar had won this competition since it began competing in

Soccer is the favorite sport of young Tanzanians.

1947, and this is the kind of wild excitement the game receives in Tanzania!

Volleyball is becoming a popular game for men and women and the new seaside variation of beachball is starting to catch on. A few go to watch boxing or wrestling. Otherwise, apart from women's netball and a game of darts in the bar for the men, Tanzanians do not go in for many structured sports.

MARATHON

Tanzanian sportsmen excel in long-distance running. In 1978 Gidamis Shahanga was the first black African to win the Commonwealth Games marathon in Alberta, Canada. In 1980, at the Moscow Olympics, Tanzania won two silver medals: Suleiman Nyambui in the 5,000 meters and Filbert Bayi in the 3,000-meter steeplechase. In 1984 Juma Ikangaa was sixth in the marathon in the Los Angeles Olympics, and in September 1986, he won the Tokyo marathon in 2 hours 8 minutes 10 seconds—the 10th fastest time for the marathon in the history of the event. Then in 1989, the amazing Ikangaa won the New York marathon in a new record time of 2 hours 8 minutes 1 second.

TANZANIA SCOUTS ASSOCIATION

The Boy Scout movement in Tanzania was founded in 1929 and now has over 13,000 members. Scouts (and Guides) in Tanzania follow the same sort of self-reliance program that lay behind the *ujamaa* villages. Tanzanian Scouts are far more active in community service than their brother Scouts in some other countries. In the spirit of the universal Scout motto, *Uwe tayari* ("OO-wee TAY-AR-EE"), or "Be prepared," they "learn by doing" in connection with many health and conservation projects. For example, in 1994, the Tanzania Scouts Association launched a campaign to publicize health knowledge in collaboration with UNICEF and the Ministry of Health. Scouts traveled door-to-door demonstrating to mothers how to prepare oral rehydration salts and explaining how to prevent diarrhea. They reinforced the message with puppet shows and plays. More recently, Scouts have worked in refugee camps, building shelters and helping to feed malnourished children.

Riding over the Serengeti in a hot-air balloon. The balloon is colored brown to avoid startling the animals.

WEALTHIER INDULGENCES

Some Tanzanians visit the game parks—where they pay a much lower fee for entry, guides, and accommodation than overseas visitors. It is possible to book a camel safari across the Serengeti or even to indulge in a balloon ride above the wildlife, enjoying a champagne breakfast after the flight. Around the country there are also facilities for playing tennis or golf.

FESTIVALS

IN THE COUNTRYSIDE, the pattern of life is mostly adjusted to fit with religious festivals, which tend to be Christian ones in inland Tanzania. The people of the coastal towns are mostly Muslim, so they celebrate Islamic festivals such as Eid el-Fitr and the Prophet's birthday, along with political holidays, the latter usually with parades. In addition, people celebrate important life-cycle events such as weddings, coming-of-age rites, funerals, and the harvest, often with dancing and music. Some traditional customs are maintained complete with elaborate masks and traditional dances, while others have been replaced, often by Christian customs. The majority of Tanzanians make their living by growing crops or by tending animals so festivities have to accommodate chores as well. Cows waiting to be milked cannot be ignored just because the day is officially a public holiday.

Left: **Young Makua boys receive money on their initiation day.**

Opposite: **A Makonde dancer wearing a painted mask.**

NATIONAL HOLIDAYS

New Year's Day is a holiday almost everywhere in the world. In Tanzania as well, people wait for the church bells to ring at midnight, and then good luck toasts are drunk for the new year ahead. January 1 is a public holiday.

Also in January, on the 12th, the people of Zanzibar celebrate their own independence achieved in the Revolution of 1964.

In February the dominant CCM party waves its banners and political promises during a day of parades and speeches called Chama Cha Mapinduzi Day. Then in April come the festivities of Union Day in recognition of the joining of Tanganyika and Zanzibar into the United Republic of Tanzania on April 26, 1964. Most schools prepare special celebrations for this day. More political rallies and processions, particularly on behalf of the workers and the poorer people, take place on May Day and Peasants' Day. No longer a celebration of country customs, May Day (or Labor Day) around the world has become linked with industrial achievements and trade unions. The latter are now legal in Tanzania after having been forbidden for a long time.

Independence Day in December is another grand public holiday like Union Day, celebrating

Tanzania's independence from Great Britain which was granted in 1961. With Christmas in sight and the students on vacation, this is a chance for parties and processions, festivities and fireworks.

NATIONAL ANTHEM

The Tanzanian national anthem is *Mungu Ibariki Afrika* (God Bless Africa), which has essentially the same tune and words as *Nkosi Sikelel'i Afrika*, chosen by the African National Congress (ANC) as the anthem for the newly democratic South Africa. This song is also used as the national anthem for the countries of Zambia, Namibia, and Zimbabwe. The words were written in 1867 by Enoch Sontonga, a teacher in a Methodist mission in South Africa.

PUBLIC HOLIDAYS

January 1	New Year's Day
January 12	Zanzibar Revolution Day
February 5	Chama Cha Mapinduzi (CCM) Day
April 26	Union Day
May 1	International Labor Day
July 7	Saba Saba Peasants' Day
December 9	Independence Day
December 25-26	Christmas and Boxing Days
variable	Easter
variable*	Eid el-Fitr, end of Ramadan
variable*	Islamic New Year
variable*	Birth of the Prophet

*based on the Islamic lunar calendar

Opposite: **Uhuru celebrations.**

CHRISTIAN OBSERVANCES

The two greatest festivals of the Christian year are Christmas, a rejoicing for the birth of Jesus Christ, and the days around Easter, the time at which Christians believe Christ died and rose again from the dead. These are colorful celebrations whether in the cities or in the villages.

CHRISTMAS Centered as it is on a newborn baby, Christmas has always been a happy festival for children. In a Christian Tanzanian home, families give whatever presents they can afford, particularly new clothes to the children. Everyone attends the morning service in church where the

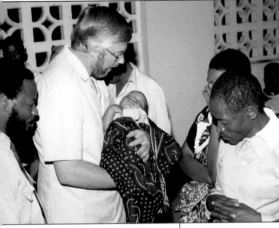

Above: **Blessing a baby during a dedication service in Tanga.**

Right: **A song leader in Elim Pentecostal Church.**

children sing the carols they have practiced (*Silent Night* is often one of them). Afterwards there is usually some kind of local celebration—in a village, this might be a communal meal for church members at someone's house, while in town, there may be dances or sports events that have taken weeks of planning.

EASTERTIDE Eastertide starts with Palm Sunday, when processions with people waving palms make their way to the churches, recalling the triumphal entry Jesus made at Jerusalem.

On Good Friday comes the solemn memory of Christ's crucifixion—a day to make the joyful massed singing on Easter Sunday even happier. The European custom of giving Easter eggs has been adopted by those Tanzanians who can afford the expensive chocolate.

A food and fun fair marks an Eid.

The Ismaili Jama'at Khana in Dar es Salaam is a religious center for Ismaili Muslims, and during Islamic festivals or on the Aga Khan's birthday it is lighted up with strings of colored lights.

MUSLIM FESTIVALS

The festivals of Islam are timed according to local sightings of various phases of the moon, so they start on different days each year. Muslims take their religious duties and celebrations very seriously. For example, the tradition of giving food, clothes, and money to the poor is an important part of all Islamic festivals.

RAMADAN During the month of *Ramadan* ("RAM-ah-dahn"), all adult Muslims fast from sunrise to sunset. *Iftar* ("EEF-tar") is the first meal that a Muslim eats after a day's fasting. The word means "breakfast" in its original sense: to break one's fast. The Prophet Mohammed broke his fast with a few dates soaked in milk, so a typical *iftar* includes dates or sweet fruit juice. Many restaurants in the Muslim parts of Tanzania are closed in the daytime during Ramadan, and normal business procedures are often interrupted.

EID EL-FITR This festival falls at the end of Ramadan. Tanzanian Muslim children enjoy helping their mother cook the sweet biscuits known as *kahk* (KAHK) to eat and give to the poor. The Prophet Mohammed celebrated the end of the fasting month by putting on his best clothes, giving charity to the poor, and going to the mosque. All Muslims therefore continue that custom.

In Zanzibar, at Eid el-Fitr, the people have a custom of their own, however. The men from the south of town challenge those from the north to a contest with banana branches. When the men are sufficiently bruised and exhausted, the women sing traditional folk songs, and everyone eats and dances until late in the night.

THE PROPHET'S BIRTHDAY On the birthday of Prophet Mohammed, *Moulid en-Nabi*, there are special services with recitations from the Koran. To show how sweet Koranic words are, the children are given boxes of candy often made of nuts.

Dancers in Ujiji on Lake Tanganyika.

FAMILY CELEBRATIONS

The influence of the mission churches has stopped many traditional family-based ceremonies. Weddings and funerals now take place in church. Baptisms may occur indoors or in a river. Even those who do not go to church are beginning to forget the old ways.

The traditional custom of funeral dances has lasted longer. Even after a church funeral, family mourners feel the need to join together in a common expression of sadness. The insistent rhythm of the drums sets people dancing silently and solemnly. Children may dance in small groups of their own. All the time the drums keep their beat, broken occasionally by groups of wind instruments wailing in a manner close to crying.

For a wedding a fresh kanga, *or robe, is essential, and young girls are often given their first* kanga *to mark the beginning of puberty.*

111

TRIBAL RITUALS

MASAI   The time when a boy "becomes a man" is exciting in any culture anywhere in the world. The people of Africa have their own customs and celebrations, often involving an initiation test for the youth to prove his manhood. Below is a description of the path a Masai follows as he progresses from boy to warrior to elder.

When still only 4 or 5, a Masai boy may have two teeth removed from his lower jaw. This custom has its beginnings in the danger in a totally outdoor life of contracting tetanus from an infected cut. In a case of bad infection, the neck and jaw muscles tighten in a condition known as lockjaw, but a child with a gap in the teeth can still be fed.

When he is about 6, the boy's earlobes are pierced for distinctive bone or metal earrings. At the onset of puberty, together with other boys his age, he receives the instruction due to him before his ritual initiation through circumcision. The operation is conducted without anesthetic, and the boy is expected to make no sound. Instead, his mother and relatives wail and yell for the pain he is enduring. This is the time of the *eunoto* ("ee-oo-NOH-toh") feast to celebrate "coming of age." A fattened bull is killed, its throat slit, and the blood mixed with milk is sipped by all to share its strength. (The government tried to ban this custom in 1973 but the decree was never enforced.)

Now the boy is ready to become a *moran*, one of the young warriors responsible for protecting the Masai cattle from thieves and wild beasts. He may carry black patterns on his shield of buffalo or giraffe hide, and braid his hair in elaborate pigtails. If he is chosen as the leader of the *moran*, he will have already proved himself as an accepted judge within the group.

At the age of about 20, he becomes a senior warrior. Not until then is he allowed to paint red ochre on his shield and perhaps be given the honor of the lion's mane headdress. The right to wear this was traditionally earned by the *moran* who took the main force of the lion's charge or who made the fatal thrust. Now that lion-hunting is forbidden, some Masai groups award this right to the warrior they consider the bravest.

The next stage is to be admitted as a junior elder, a *moruo* ("MOR-oo-oo"), when he is allowed to marry. If he is chosen later to join the ranks of the senior elders, he is one of those who are revered by the whole community and make all major decisions.

When he dies, his body will be placed in the bush to be eaten by wild animals. Only the most distinguished elders and those considered as Masai prophets (*loibons*) are buried.

MAKONDE During the dry season of the year, between June and October, curious things start happening in the Makonde villages. A farewell ceremony will be held for a number of men who have announced that they must "go away."

Their village meanwhile prepares for the Midimu ("me-DEE-mu"), which may be in celebration of a large harvest or new fields being planted for the first time, or it may be the end of the initiation instruction for the boys and girls. Everyone waits eagerly for the night when, under a waxing moon, the masked and therefore unrecognizable Midimu dancers come bounding out of the darkness with drums throbbing and lighted torches waving. All the villagers burst out of their houses to join them. That is the beginning of a feast that continues for three days and nights.

Eventually the "missing" men, all professional dancers and musicians, return home. Everyone knows why they have been away, but nothing is ever said. Behind their Midimu masks, they were unrecognizable while dancing, as if invisible.

FOOD

TAPPING A MIXTURE OF African, Indian, and Arab influences, inventive Tanzanian cooks combine foods in unusual ways. Their staple foods are common with those eaten elsewhere in Africa—corn, cassava, rice, plantains, beans, okra, and coconuts as well as (depending on the region and the ability to afford it) beef, chicken, goat meat, and seafood. A wide variety of fruit is available, including papayas, mangoes, bananas, pineapples, and watermelon.

In many Tanzanian homes, breakfast is a simple meal of bread and butter, though some enjoy *mandazi* ("man-DAH-zee"), a kind of deep-fried doughnut that goes well with their sweet tea. Lunch is usually the main meal of the day: a solid serving of something starchy, such as a porridge called *ugali* ("oo-GAH-lee"), cassava, or rice, served with beans, pumpkin, or *mchicha* ("m-CHEE-CHAH") greens. There may also be a small helping of grilled beef or fish. The evening meal is usually light.

The basic aim of most Tanzanian food is that it should be as filling as possible and as cheap as possible. Meat, which is expensive, is often used just as a flavoring rather than as a main ingredient.

Left: **A vegetable market in Stone Town, Zanzibar.**

Opposite: **Homemade beer being sold in the market.**

115

UGALI

Ugali is a stiff porridge, usually of corn, and is the main ingredient of the menu for 90% of Tanzanians. Since it is not expensive, people can usually afford something to go with it, such as meat, beans, or spinach, and so be sure of one satisfying and fairly balanced meal each day. The housewife starts with the raw grain and pounds it in a mortar before making it into a thick paste with a little water. Then it is added to a large pot of boiling water and boiled until it thickens to form a thick dough. The cook needs a strong arm and a sturdy spoon to stir the mixture. *Ugali* can be eaten hot or left to cool then cut into slices and fried. Another method is to make holes in the warm *ugali* with a small ladle and fill these with soup or meat. That way both keep warm longer.

Although usually made from corn, *ugali* is also cooked from cassava, millet, or sorghum.

MAKING UGALI

1 ³/₄ pints (1 liter) water, or water and milk to make it creamier
2 ounces (60 g) butter or margerine
1 pound (500 g) cornflour
salt

Mix half the flour and about a quarter of the water in a bowl with a wooden spoon until it is a smooth paste. Boil the rest of the water with the butter and a pinch of salt, and then add the paste, stirring steadily for at least a minute and bringing it back to a boil. Then add the rest of the flour a little at a time while you keep on stirring—you will understand how strong Tanzanian cooks must be! Keep going until the mixture has turned into a stiff dough. (You can add a little more flour or a little more water if necessary. The mixture should not stick to the pot.)

BANANAS

There are at least 17 different varieties of banana in Tanzania and probably up to 170 different ways of cooking them. They are usually eaten for the evening meal. In addition there are the larger, slightly tougher banana-like plantains. Menus can include banana soup, roast bananas served on banana leaves, banana and coconut stew, fried banana chips (more popular than potatoes), banana cream as dessert, or fried banana fritters. People also like to drink banana wine sipped through grass straws. As well as feasting on assorted bananas, the Tanzanians use banana leaves to thatch their homes or simply as an inexpensive umbrella.

Different regions have their own specialities. The creamy banana (or plantain) soup known as *mtory* ("um-TOR-ee") is fed to nursing mothers in the Kilimanjaro region. (And to their husbands when no one is looking!) It is made from beef and bones, green bananas or plantains, with onion and tomato.

VILLAGE COOKING

A woman pounding cassava.

The village housewife manages without an electric stove or a refrigerator. Her washing machine is probably the eldest daughter! Yet on a paraffin stove or a simple fire of wood and charcoal she can create cakes, buns, doughnuts, flat cakes, rice-flour bread, stews, meatballs, and of course *ugali.* Fruit and vegetables come fresh from the vegetable patch or the market. Cassava and *mchicha* are common vegetables. *Mchicha,* a leafy green, is eaten by everyone in Tanzania because it is cheap and grows everywhere including backyards. Meat or fish, when it can be afforded, is either smoked and dried or freshly caught or killed. For a rare feast, *ndayu* ("un-DAY-oo"), a roasted young goat, is a popular delicacy throughout the country.

The housewife's utensils include a mortar and pestle, plastic water containers, some bowls and jugs, a tin sheet for bread or biscuits, and cooking pots made of both aluminum and pottery because she believes certain foods taste better when cooked in clay pots, while tea is better out of aluminum. Many households don't bother with knives and forks; they use fingers for eating, plus a spoon when required.

To smoke meat is a lengthy procedure. The traditional way is to dig a deep pit in the ground and then lay felled trees in it with their leafy branches spread out in thick layers. The meat is cut lengthwise, washed and salted, then laid neatly on the leaves. The fire is lit and the smoke cures the meat, while at least one person keeps a careful watch to make sure the fire does not flare and scorch the meat.

WATERSIDE FOOD

Those fortunate enough to live beside the Indian Ocean or on the shores of one of the Great Lakes may be able to add varieties of fish or seafood to their diet as a welcome change. On Lake Tanganyika fishermen go out at night with lights hung from the prow of the boat to attract the small, sardine-like fish known as *dagaa* ("da-GAH") to the surface. A sudden beating of drums scares them into momentary stillness before nets scoop them up. Fried fresh or dried in the sun, they form a tasty source of protein. Lake Victoria has large, favored Nile perch. The ocean is rich too, in lobsters, crabs, kingfish, and other creatures. Even the poorest can gather crabs or clams when the tide goes out, then boil them in a pot with peeled cassava. Prawns are popularly served hot and spicy, flavored with garlic. Restaurants serve a famous coconut fish curry, *samaki wa nazi* ("sah-MAH-kee wah NAH-zee").

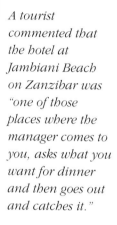

A tourist commented that the hotel at Jambiani Beach on Zanzibar was "one of those places where the manager comes to you, asks what you want for dinner and then goes out and catches it."

Boys with a fresh catch from the sea.

DRINKS

The most common drink in Tanzania is tea—although the people have their own special way of making it. Tea leaves and sugar are boiled together, sometimes with the addition of cardamom seeds or ginger, and the result is called *chai* ("CHAH-ee"). Tanzanians drink it with or without milk. Curiously, though they grow and export excellent coffee, they do not drink much of it themselves. Visitors are usually served black tea sprinkled with ginger powder.

Coconut milk comes fresh, but the abundant and cheap fruit is seldom made into juice in this country, possibly because this would involve discarding the wholesome flesh of the fruit.

Those wanting an alcoholic drink have the choice of beer or *konyagi* ("kon-YAH-gee"), which is a spirit made from sugarcane. Bottled beer is likely to be Safari or Pilsner; home-brewed beer is called *pombe* ("POM-beh"). Imported beers from across the nearest border (Kenya, Malawi, and the Democratic Republic of Congo) are also popular.

EATING OUT

There are countless small-town restaurants called *hotelis* ("ho-TELL-ees") that usually serve some sort of stew based on rice or *ugali* or boiled plantain. This is served together with chicken, beef, or goat or simply with a mixture of beans. Food stalls in the street sell *mishkaki* ("mish-KAH-ki"), which are kebabs of goat or stringy beef, barbecued chicken, triangular spicy samosas, and dangerously hot chili bites called *bhajias* ("bah-GEE-ahs"). When the British empire arrived in Tanzania, so did the idea of chips or fries. Now potatoes are fried everywhere and passers-by can feast on *chipsi na mayai* (chips and egg) or *chipsi na kuku* (chips and chicken).

Tanzanians delight in dabaga *sauce, a fiery chili sauce produced in Dabaga, near Iringa.*

Food vendors of inexpensive meals are prevalent in the city.

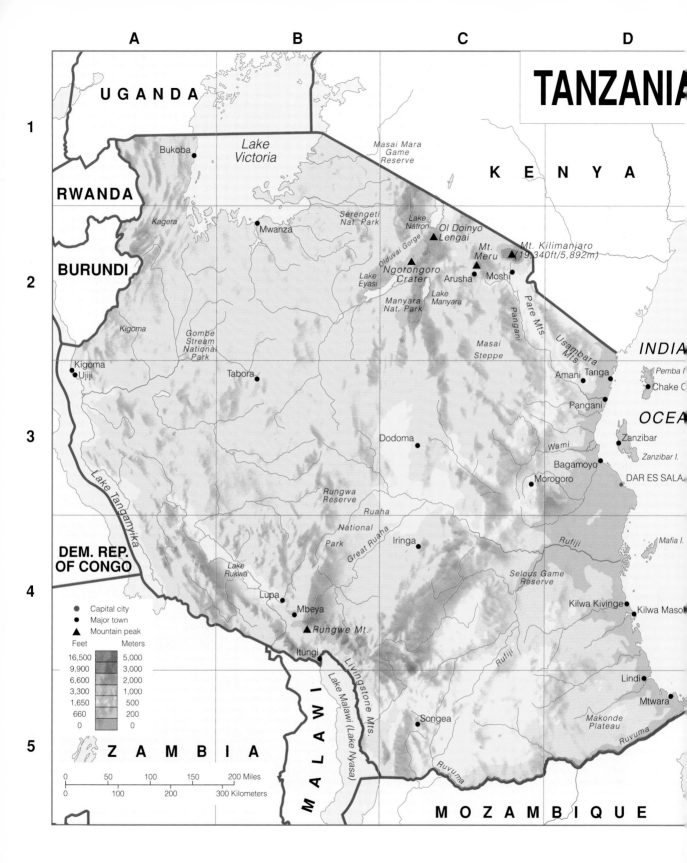

TANZANIA

A   B   C   D

1

UGANDA

Lake Victoria

Bukoba

Masai Mara Game Reserve

RWANDA

K E N Y A

Kagera

Mwanza

2

BURUNDI

Serengeti Nat. Park

Lake Natron

Ol Doinyo Lengai ▲

Mt. Meru ▲

Mt. Kilimanjaro ▲ *(19,340ft/5,892m)*

Olduvai Gorge

Ngorongoro Crater ▲

Arusha ● ● Moshi

Lake Eyasi

Lake Manyara

Manyara Nat. Park

Masai Steppe

Kigoma

Gombe Stream National Park

Pangani

Pare Mts.

Usambara Mts.

INDIA

Kigoma ●
Ujiji ●

Tabora ●

Amani ● ● Tanga

OCEA

Pemba I

● Chake C

Pangani ●

3

Lake Tanganyika

Dodoma ●

Wami

● Zanzibar

Zanzibar I.

Bagamoyo ●

DAR ES SALA

Morogoro ●

Rungwa Reserve

Ruaha

National Park

Great Ruaha

Iringa ●

Rufiji

Mafia I.

DEM. REP. OF CONGO

Lake Rukwa

Selous Game Reserve

4

Lupa ●

Mbeya ●

Kilwa Kivinge ● ● Kilwa Maso

▲ *Rungwe Mt.*

Itungi ●

Rufiji

● Lindi

● Mtwara

Songea ●

Makonde Plateau

Ruvuma

5

Z A M B I A

M A L A W I

Lake Malawi (Lake Nyasa)

Livingstone Mts.

Ruvuma

M O Z A M B I Q U E

● Capital city
● Major town
▲ Mountain peak

Feet	Meters
16,500	5,000
9,900	3,000
6,600	2,000
3,300	1,000
1,650	500
660	200
0	0

0   50   100   150   200 Miles

0   100   200   300 Kilometers

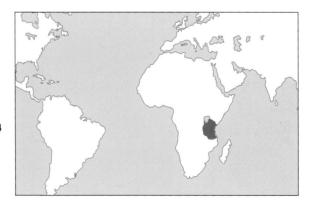

QUICK NOTES

OFFICIAL NAME
United Republic of Tanzania
Jamburi ya Muungano wa Tanzania

LAND AREA
364,900 square miles (945,090 square km)

POPULATION
29,700,000 (1995 estimate)

CAPITAL
Dar es Salaam

IMPORTANT CITIES
Dodoma, Mwanza, Arusha, Tanga, Zanzibar

NATIONAL FLAG
Green and blue, divided by a diagonal black stripe bordered with gold.

MAJOR RIVERS
Rufiji, Pangani, Wami, Ruvuma

MAJOR LAKES
Victoria, Tanganyika, Malawi (Nyasa)

HIGHEST POINT
Mount Kilimanjaro (19,340 feet/5,892 m)

NATIONAL LANGUAGES
Kiswahili and English

BIRTH RATE
4.5%

LIFE EXPECTANCY
Female 55; male 50

MAJOR RELIGIONS
Christianity, Islam, Hinduism, and traditional beliefs

CURRENCY
Tanzanian shilling (650 Tsh = US$1)

MAIN EXPORTS
Coffee, cotton, diamonds, tobacco, tea, sisal, and cloves

RELIGIOUS HOLIDAYS
Christmas, Easter, Eid el-Fitr

MAJOR NATIONAL HOLIDAYS
Union Day (April 26) celebrating the union of Tanganyika and Zanzibar to form Tanzania.
Independence Day (December 9)
Zanzibar Revolution Day (January 12)

POLITICAL LEADERS
Julius Nyerere (President 1961–85)
Ali Hassan Mwinyi (President 1985–96)
Benjamin Mkapa (President 1996–)
Salim Amour (President of Zanzibar)

GOVERNMENT
CCM is the ruling party.
CUF, CHADEMA, MDA, and NCCR-Mageuzi are other major political parties.
Elections are held every five years.

MAIN GROUPS
Sukuma, Nyamwezi, Hehe, Chaga, Makonde, Gogo, Masai, Haya, Ha, and Swahili

LITERACY
68% of the population

GLOSSARY

Bantu ("BAN-too")
Describes African tribes originally from the Niger-Congo region that all speak a common group of languages.

bao ("BAH-oh")
Traditional African game played with beans or pebbles on a wooden board with two parallel rows of holes.

bride-wealth
Money or goods paid by a prospective husband.

bui-bui ("BOO-ee BOO-ee")
Head-covering worn by some Muslim women.

bwana ("BWAH-nah")
A term of respect used for men that literally means "father of many sons."

iftar ("EEF-tar")
The first meal a Muslim eats when breaking his or her fast at sunset.

jambo ("YAM-boh")
Greeting used by Tanzanians.

kanga ("KAN-gah")
Robe or wrap, usually brightly colored.

kanzu ("KAN-zoo")
Ankle-length robe worn by Muslim men.

Kiswahili ("ki-swah-HEE-lee")
The official language of Tanzania, derived primarily from a mixture of Bantu and Arab words as spoken on the coast.

matatu ("ma-TAH-too")
Minibus taxi.

mchicha ("m-CHEE-CHAH")
A green vegetable, rather like spinach.

miombo ("mee-OM-bo")
Woodlands with only a sparse cover of trees.

moran ("MO-RAHN")
A young Masai warrior.

moruo ("MOR-oo-oo")
A junior elder among the Masai.

mzee ("m-ZEE")
A term of respect used by younger to older.

Ngai ("ung-EYE")
The god of the Masai.

ngomas ("un-GOH-mahs")
Traditional dances.

pombe ("POM-beh")
Home-brewed beer.

Ramadan
The month of fasting for Muslims.

rift valleys
Volcanic splits in the earth's surface.

tembo ("TEM-boh")
Alcoholic drink produced from coconuts.

ugali ("oo-GAH-lee")
A stiff porridge made usually of corn and a main part of the meal for most Tanzanians.

ujamaa ("oo-JAH-mah")
The concept of state-controlled community villages

BIBLIOGRAPHY

Amin, Mohammed, D.C. Willotts, and J. Eames. *The Last of the Masaai.* Cape Town: Struik, 1987.

Briggs, Philip. *Guide to Tanzania.* England: Bradt Publications, 1993.

Hafner, Dorinda. *A Taste of Africa.* California: Ten Speed Press, 1993.

Mercer, Graham. *Tanzania.* London: Globetrotter, 1996.

Murray, Jocelyn. *Cultural Atlas of Africa.* New York: Facts on File, 1981.

INDEX

INDEX

INDEX

PICTURE CREDITS